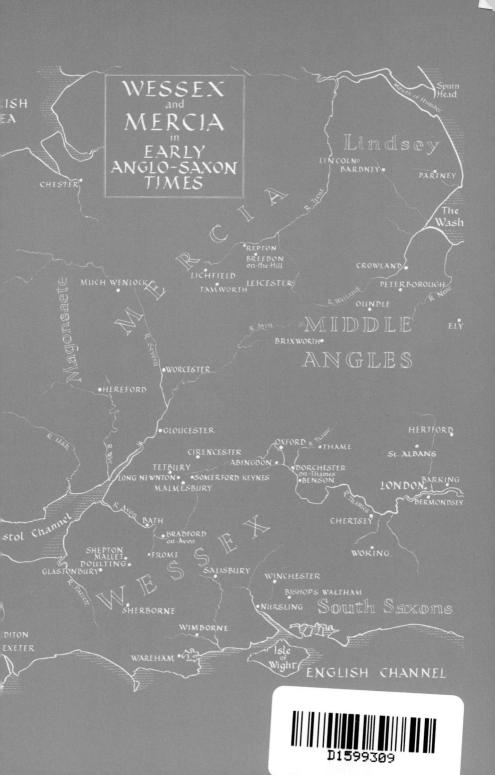

WESSEX
and
MERCIA
in
EARLY
ANGLO-SAXON
TIMES

LISH
EA

CHESTER

M E R C I A

Magonsaete

MUCH WENLOCK

HEREFORD

WORCESTER

R. Severn

R. Wye

R. Usk

GLOUCESTER

CIRENCESTER

TETBURY

LONG NEWTON • • SOMERFORD KEYNES

MALMESBURY

R. Avon

BATH

BRADFORD
on-Avon

SHEPTON
MALLET
DOULTING • • FROME

GLASTONBURY

R. Parret

SHEPTON

SHERBORNE

W E S S E X

Lindsey

LINCOLN○
BARDNEY

PARTNEY

The
Wash

Spurn
Head

Mouth of Humber

R. Trent

REPTON
BREEDON
on-the-Hill

LICHFIELD
TAMWORTH

LEICESTER

CROWLAND

PETERBOROUGH

R. Nene

R. Welland

OUNDLE

ELY

R. Avon

BRIXWORTH

MIDDLE

ANGLES

HERTFORD

OXFORD R. Thame

THAME

St. ALBANS

ABINGDON

DORCHESTER
on-Thames
BENSON

R. Thames

LONDON

BARKING

BERMONDSEY

CHERTSEY

WOKING

SALISBURY

WINCHESTER

BISHOP'S WALTHAM

NURSLING

South Saxons

WIMBORNE

DITON
EXETER

WAREHAM

Isle
of
Wight

ENGLISH CHANNEL

stol Channel

THE EARLY CHURCH IN WESSEX AND MERCIA

Other Books by Margaret Gallyon

The Early Church in Eastern England
The Early Church in Northumbria

THE EARLY CHURCH
IN WESSEX AND MERCIA

by

MARGARET GALLYON

TERENCE DALTON LIMITED
LAVENHAM . SUFFOLK
1980

Published by
TERENCE DALTON LIMITED
ISBN 0 900963 58 1

274.22
G139

82010816

Text photoset in 11/12 pt. Baskerville

Printed in Great Britain at
THE LAVENHAM PRESS LIMITED
LAVENHAM   .   SUFFOLK

Contents

Index of Illustrations

Preface

THIS THIRD book on the Early English Church completes a study of the stages by which Christianity reached the various kingdoms of the Anglo-Saxons in the seventh and eighth centuries. The first book dealt with the conversion of Kent, Sussex, East Anglia and Essex, the second with Northumbria. The present volume describes the coming of the Faith to the kingdoms of Wessex and Mercia.

To a race of warring tribes and rival kingdoms Christianity came as a unifying and civilizing force. It brought with it not only a religion of high moral precepts, intellectual appeal and deep spirituality, but also an entirely new culture. This was derived chiefly from the Celtic culture of Ireland and from that of the Continent, particularly of Italy and Gaul, from where many of the early missionaries came. The new culture, with its emphasis on education and learning, did not destroy the Anglo-Saxon's own indigenous culture but enhanced and enriched it, the fusion of the two producing works of great artistic and literary achievement.

As with the rest of the English kingdoms it was through the monasteries that this new religion and culture reached the pagan tribes of Wessex and Mercia. With the coming of the monks and clergy an interaction was established between the Church and society. The secular rulers encouraged the work of the clergy, donating land for churches and monasteries. The Church in turn supported the secular rulers and influenced every aspect of society giving it new insights and perspectives. Nowhere better is this seen than in the contribution of Churchmen towards the reshaping of traditional codes of law which, with the introduction of religion, was infused with a new spirit of humanity and enlightenment.

Of the two kingdoms dealt with in this book, Wessex was to emerge as pre-eminent and, eventually, through the leadership of Alfred the Great, to bring unity to the English people. It is from the royal house of Wessex that our own royal family traces its origin. In the field of religion, too, Wessex can claim renown among the English kingdoms for its missionary enterprise, resulting in the exodus of great numbers of men and women from that kingdom into the mission fields of northern and central Europe.

The most celebrated of the West Saxon missionaries was Boniface of Devon who converted the pagan tribes of Thuringia,

Hesse and Bavaria and died a martyr's death in Friesland. As patron saint of Germany his name is commemorated in a wealth of church dedications in that country and in many parts of Europe. But in England he is little known and few churches honour him in their dedications. The year of 1980, however, saw the thirteenth centenary of the saint's birth. In the diocese of Exeter, and in Crediton in particular, the place of his birth, an impressive programme of events took place. It is to be hoped that these celebrations will have helped to make this great Englishman more widely known in the country of his origin.

Any student of this early period of English history acknowledges the debt he owes to the Venerable Bede, the eighth century historian, without whose work we should know little of Dark Age Britain. In my study of this period his *History of the English Church and People* has been my constant companion and forms the framework of my three books. To him and to all other writers of this period, past and present, whose books I have used, I wish to express my thanks. I acknowledge with appreciation also the many others who have helped with the production of the books; and, with this present volume, in particular, I thank Miss Nancie Pelling for drawing the map, Mr. R. N. Gallyon for correcting the manuscript in rough draft, Professor H. Mayr-Harting for reading the typescript and making a number of useful comments, and all those who have supplied me with illustrations or information.

Margaret Gallyon
Cambridge
July 1980

Main dates relating to the Early History of Wessex

495 Chieftains Cerdic and Cynric landed in Britain
519 They obtained the kingdom of Wessex
534 Death of Cerdic. Accession of Cynric
560 Death of Cynric. Accession of King Ceawlin
593 Death of Ceawlin followed by short reigns of various kings
611 Accession of King Cynigils
634 Arrival of Bishop Birinus in Wessex
635 Cynigils baptised. Malmesbury Abbey founded by Maelduib
636 King Cwichelm baptised
639 Birth of Aldhelm
641 Accession of King Cenwalh
648 Dedication of Old Minster, Winchester
650 Death of Bishop Birinus. Agilbert, the Frank, bishop of Wessex
655 Deusdedit consecrated archbishop of Canterbury
660 Agilbert resigned. Bishop Wini appointed Bishop
663 Bishop Wini driven out by King Cenwalh
670 Leutherius consecrated bishop of Wessex
672 Death of King Cenwalh followed by reigns of Queen Sexburg, King Centwini and other sub-kings
676 Haeddi appointed bishop of Wessex
685 Cadwalla contending for the kingdom. Became king
688 Cadwalla abdicated and went to Rome. Ine king
705 West Saxon diocese divided
709 Death of Aldhelm
718 Boniface sets out for Frisia
722 Boniface consecrated bishop
726 King Ine retired to Rome. Accession of King Ethelheard
741 Willibald consecrated bishop of Eichstatt
754 Martyrdom of Boniface
780 Death of Abbess Leoba

Main dates relating to the Early History of Mercia

626 Accession of King Penda
632 King Edwin of Northumbria killed by Penda and Cadwallon
641 King Oswald of Northumbria killed by Penda
653 King Peada, son of Penda, converted to Christianity. Ruler of Middle Anglia.
655 Battle of Winwaed. Penda killed. Peada, king of Mercia.
656 (or 7) Murder of Peada
657 Accession of King Wulfhere
659 Trumhere appointed bishop of Mercia
662 Death of Trumhere. Jarumen appointed bishop
667 Death of Jarumen
669 Chad appointed bishop of Mercia
672 Death of Chad. Consecration of Wynfrith. Council of Hertford
675 Death of Wulfhere. Accession of King Ethelred
     Deposition of Wynfrith. Sexwulf became bishop of Mercia.
679 Battle of Trent
680 Council of Hatfield
691 Headda appointed bishop of Mercia
697 Murder of Queen Osthryth
704 King Ethelred became a monk at Bardney. Accession of Coenred
709 Coenred abdicated and went to Rome. Accession of Ceolred
716 Death of Ceolred. Accession of King Aethelbald

CHAPTER ONE

St Birinus, Apostle of Wessex

TO THE Saxon tribes who invaded south west Britain and whose way of life lay rooted in the soil, the area must have seemed a desirable acquisition. Its fertile soil and rich pastures, its rolling hills, chalk downs, forests and rivers provided ample scope for their rural activities. Here they could grow their crops of barley and wheat, pasture their sheep and cattle and catch an abundance of fish and fowl. The great forest of Selwood which ran from north to south along the Wiltshire-Somerset border provided the settlers with plentiful supplies of timber, their chief building material, and with fuel for burning. In the forests too there was pannage for their swine, acorns and beech mast.

In the seventh century Gloucester and the surrounding district had been conquered by the Saxons. It was an agricultural paradise, typical of much of south west Britain. William of Malmesbury, the twelfth century historian and chronicler, describes the Vale of Gloucester thus: "the soil is rich in corn and fertile in fruit . . . if anyone is disposed to be lazy, mere avarice will tempt him to the joys of labour, where labour is rewarded by the return of a hundredfold. The river Severn adds to the glory of the district. No river in the whole land is wider in its channel, more vehement in its current, more responsive to the art of the fisherman."*

The West Saxon kingdom in the seventh and eighth centuries roughly covered the present day counties of Berkshire, Oxfordshire, Hampshire, Wiltshire, Dorset and most of Gloucestershire, Somerset and Devon. Its extent fluctuated, of course, as did the other major English kingdoms, according to the territorial gains and losses it sustained in battles against neighbouring tribes. The forest of Selwood provided a natural defence against the Britons to the west and in the eighth century it separated the two West Saxon dioceses, Sherborne to the west of Selwood and Winchester to the east. In the ninth century the forest provided a refuge for Alfred the Great and

---

* *St Aldhelm, His Life and Times.* G. F. Browne

his fighting men as they prepared for renewed attacks against the Danish army.

The West Saxon dynasty is the most complicated of all the royal houses of early England. A few prominent names emerge, however, and upon these we shall concentrate in this study. The first to be mentioned in the *Anglo-Saxon Chronicle* are the two Saxon chieftains, Cerdic and his son, Cynric, who, with five shiploads of warriors landed at Certicesora, thought to have been in the Southampton area, in the year 495. They fought against the native Britons, or the Welsh as they are sometimes called, and in 508 killed the British king, Natanleod, and five thousand of his men. In 530 they conquered the Isle of Wight and in 534 Cerdic, who was regarded as the founder of the West Saxon kingdom, died. It is to Cerdic and the royal house of Wessex that genealogists trace the ancestry of our present royal family.

Cerdic was succeeded by his son, Cynric, whose reign covered the years 534 to 560. Conquests under his leadership were made at Old Sarum and Barbary Castle. After his death in 560 his son Ceawlin emerges as the dominant ruler of the West Saxons. His long reign of about thirty years is marked by further territorial gains for the Saxons against the Britons. These included Durham, Gloucester, Cirencester and Bath with many villages and much spoil. His pre-eminence among contemporary kings is noted by Bede in his *History of the English Church and People*. Ceawlin is the second in a list of seven powerful rulers who gained overlordship over all the kingdoms south of the Humber, the first being Aelle, king of the South Saxons, in the district we know as Sussex.

After the death of Ceawlin the succession of West Saxon kings is confused and their origin uncertain. Only with the beginning of the reign of Cynigils in 611 can we enter the realm of history and turn from the bare bones of the *Anglo-Saxon Chronicle* to the more fleshy narrative of the eighth century historian, Bede. In his *Ecclesiastical History of the English People* Bede gives us some historical facts about Cynigils, but his interest in this king is only secondary to his interest in the religious event which occurred during his reign. This was the arrival in Wessex of the missionary St Birinus who preached the Gospel to the pagan people of this kingdom.

Even Bede's account of the conversion of Wessex is less detailed than that of the other English kingdoms, especially of Kent and Northumbria. Kent, being the first of the kingdoms to receive conversion from the Roman missionaries, had acquired a place of central importance in the history of the English Church with Canterbury as the seat of its first and succeeding archbishops. Original documents, letters and records of the conversion would have been kept at the monastery of St Peter and St Paul at Canterbury, its abbot, Albinus, having access to them so that he was able to convey information to Bede. Northumbrian history presented no problem to Bede either, since he was a native of the kingdom, had spent all his life there and had numerous friends and acquaintances to help him to verify the facts of its history. But Wessex was a great distance from him and the only contacts he mentions as having supplied him with information about its history are Albinus in Canterbury, Nothelm, a priest in London, and his friend Daniel, bishop of Winchester. Perhaps the documents and records relating to the Christian mission to the West Saxons were scanty and therefore his informants had little to tell him. Certainly Birinus seems to have been something of an independent kind of missionary. It is not certain where he came from. No mention is made of his having come with any companions, though he may have had some, and we hear nothing of his mission being undertaken under the authority, and with the backing, of the archbishop of Canterbury, Honorius.

Though Bede makes no mention of the archbishop of Canterbury in his account of Birinus' mission, he makes it clear that the pope, also named Honorius, supported his work and personally discussed with Birinus the questions as to where in Britain he should preach the Gospel. Birinus had promised the pope that he would sow the seeds of the Faith in the most inward and remote regions of England where no teacher had been before. The pope then sent Birinus to Genoa for episcopal ordination by Asterius, archbishop of Milan. This would be on Birinus' direct route northwards from Rome, through Gaul to the northern coast from where he would take a ship across the Channel to Britain. It has been suggested that Birinus may have been a Lombard by birth and a native of Genoa, alternatively that he had at some time worked in that area under Archbishop Asterius*. At Bobbio, not far from Genoa, was a large and important monastery founded by the celebrated Irish missionary, St Columbanus, who died there in 615. It is not unlikely that Birinus may have received his religious training in this monastery which was renowned for its learning, or that he had some other kind of connection with it.

---

*Saint Berin. The Apostle of Wessex. J. E. Field, S.P.C.K.

Bede's silence on the question of Birinus' mission being undertaken with or without the backing of the archbishop of Canterbury cannot be taken as evidence that he did not have this backing. If, at first, he worked independently of Canterbury it is possible that once the mission had been established, the archbishop gave his authority and support for its continuation. This same archbishop, Honorius, shortly before, had commissioned the Burgundian bishop, Felix, to preach in East Anglia. Indeed there is a similarity in the circumstances in which these two missionary bishops, Felix from Burgundy and Birinus from Genoa, arrived in Britain and preached the Faith. It is even possible that the two were acquainted before they came to Britain.

When the pope commissioned Birinus to preach in the most heathen and remote parts of Britain he perhaps had the kingdom of Mercia in mind. News of events in England were followed with interest in Rome. Pope Honorius I showed particular interest in the English mission and had written to Northumbria's king, Edwin, to encourage him and his people to persevere in their Christian discipleship. We may imagine the distress felt in Rome when news was received of Edwin's death in battle against Cadwallon, king of the Welsh and Penda, king of Mercia. If Edwin's Christian character "had been spoken of throughout the world" we may be sure that Penda's stubborn paganism was equally well known. No kingdom of the English was more in need of conversion than Penda's kingdom of Mercia.

It seemed to have been the pope's wish that Birinus should seek out fresh ground in which to sow the seeds of the Faith in England. Bede tells us that he came to the territory of the Gewissae, that is the West Saxons of south west England. Whether he landed directly in their kingdom on the south west coast, or made his way there after landing at one of the Kentish ports, we do not know. His decision to stay in this district, rather than to travel deeper into the heart of England, was prompted by his dismay at finding the Gewissae so entirely heathen. Here, if anywhere, was fresh ground in which to sow the seeds of the Faith. So Birinus stayed in Wessex and made a name for himself in the annals of history as their apostle and evangelist.

When Birinus arrived in Wessex in about 634 King Cynigils had been ruling the kingdom for over twenty years and was no longer a young man. Early in his reign he and his son, Cwichelm, had been involved in battles against the Britons and, at a place named Beandum, killed two thousand and sixty-five of their people. They had fought also against their northern neighbour, King Penda of Mercia, at Cirencester, and made a peace treaty with him. In the far north of England was the most powerful kingdom of Northumbria. In the early years of Cynigils' reign hostile relations existed between Wessex and Northumbria. Perhaps in an attempt to regain the supreme power over the southern English which their forbear, Ceawlin, had held, an assassin was sent from Cwichelm to the royal court of Northumbria to kill King Edwin, overlord of all the southern Kingdoms. It is unlikely that Cynigils was not also in some way a party to the plot, though Bede puts the blame on his son, Cwichelm. Wessex had to pay dearly for her rebellion against her overlord. The assassination attempt failed in that Edwin was only wounded and not killed. But when he had recovered he sent his army into Wessex to punish the rebels, and in the fighting five chieftains and many others were killed.

Hostilities between the two kingdoms had ceased by the time Bishop Birinus reached Wessex. Edwin had been killed by Penda's cruel army and in his place Oswald, the noblest of Northumbria's kings, reigned. He was a Christian king of deep piety but no weakling. Cadwallon, king of the Welsh, was slain by his army; Penda for a time acknowledged defeat and Oswald was established as overlord of all the kingdoms south of the Humber. Wessex, in particular, must be appeased. Oswald knew of the conflict that had existed between the two kingdoms in his predecessor's reign. He wished now to keep on friendly terms with King Cynigils. Marriage to his daughter would strengthen the peace between them. So a marriage was arranged between Oswald and Cynigils' daughter and took place during the early years of Bishop Birinus' episcopate.

We can safely assume that when Birinus came to the court of King Cynigils the king was not completely ignorant of the new religion which was being preached in almost every kingdom of the English. Despite the hazards of travel in early England, kings travelled much, not only within their own kingdoms from one royal residence to another, but also from kingdom to kingdom. Bede's *History* gives ample evidence of this. News, either through his own travel, or through the visits of others to his own court, must have reached Cynigils of what Christianity was about. By the time Birinus reached Wessex the Christian faith was already established and being practised in Northumbria, Lindsey, East Anglia and Kent; Essex, too, had heard the message but lapsed from its practice.

Cynigils therefore gladly accepted Bishop Birinus into his kingdom and gave him permission to preach to his people. Oswald of

5

Northumbria must also have encouraged the mission since he himself was a Christian and had invited missionaries from Iona to preach to his people. If King Cynigils had a vague knowledge of Christianity before Birinus came to his kingdom, it was certain now that he required a full course of instruction in its doctrines and the obligations of membership of its community. This was given to him by Bishop Birinus.

In the following year, 635, Cynigils and many of his people were baptised. We may assume that these included various members of his family, household and servants, thanes and noblemen. Cynigils' godfather was none other than his recently acquired son-in-law, King Oswald of Northumbria. "Lovely indeed and well pleasing to God was their relationship," comments Bede. For some reason Cwichelm had not been baptised on this occasion. He was baptised in the following year, 636, shortly before his death.

Cynigils wished to see his bishop firmly established in the kingdom of the West Saxons in an episcopal city of his own. With the agreement of his overlord, King Oswald, he gave Birinus the city of Dorchester-on-Thames. Here, says Bede, he built and dedicated churches and brought many people to God by his holy labours. The present day Abbey Church of St Peter and St Paul, founded in 1140, is believed to have been built on the same site as Birinus' original monastic church. In the east window of the chancel is a thirteenth century roundel depicting what is usually said to be the pope commissioning Birinus for his work among the English. Birinus is wearing a bishop's mitre. Since he was not a bishop until he had been consecrated by Archbishop Asterius of Milan, after his meeting with the pope, it is more likely that the second mitred figure is the archbishop rather than the pope. Another splendid piece of stained glass in the main east window shows Birinus preaching to the king and his people.

Dorchester, now a village, stands at the junction of the rivers Thame and Thames, between the Berkshire Downs and the Chiltern Hills. Archaeological finds in the district confirm that it was once a city of considerable size and, like the whole of the valley of the middle Thames, extensively occupied in Roman and Anglo-Saxon times. Dorchester was in the north of the West Saxon kingdom and therefore near the Mercian border. Later in the century it came into Mercian hands as is evidenced by a charter which states that King Wulfhere of Mercia had a royal estate at Thame.

Several entries in the *Anglo-Saxon Chronicle* refer to Dorchester-on-Thames. In 636 "Cwichelm was baptised at Dorchester and the same year passed away". In 639 "Birinus baptised Cuthred [son of Cwichelm] at Dorchester and stood sponsor for him". We can assume that King Cynigils was also baptised here and that the choice of a place in the north of the kingdom for the occasion was partly for the benefit of King Oswald who had to travel a great distance from Northumbria. Dorchester then became a suitable place for the two kings to meet.

Birinus was still administering the church in Wessex in the reign of Cynigils' successor, his son, Cenwalh. The *Anglo-Saxon Chronicle* records Cenwalh's succession in 641, though it may have been a year or two later than this. Cenwalh had not been among those baptised at the time of his father's baptism. He had, in fact, rejected the teaching and sacraments of the Church and infringed its laws by putting away his wife and marrying another. This was not only an offence against the Church; it incurred also the wrath of King Penda of Mercia since Cenwalh's lawful wife was Penda's sister. Penda now wreaked vengeance on Cenwalh, invading his kingdom and driving him out. In terror for his life Cenwalh fled to East Anglia and was given protection by King Anna, a devout Christian king who was giving every encouragement to Bishop Felix in the evangelisation of his country. Cenwalh had taken refuge with one of the most ardent supporters of the Faith which he himself had rejected. The influence of King Anna and his devout family soon brought about the conversion of Cenwalh for, says Bede, "Anna, his host, was a good man and blessed with good and holy children." Anna's daughters were to achieve fame as nuns and abbesses of religious houses in both England and France. The best known of these was Etheldreda, founder of the minster at Ely in the fens of East Anglia. She was about thirteen or so when King Cenwalh was an exile in her father's court. We may surmise that many hours were spent by the two kings conversing upon the question of religion. Bishop Felix, as well as King Anna, no doubt had an influence upon Cenwalh, inducing him to accept the Faith. Florence of Worcester, a twelfth century chronicler, records that Cenwalh was baptised by Bishop Felix and that Anna stood as his godfather.

In 647, or the year following, Cenwalh was restored to his West Saxon kingdom. We now find him supporting the advancement of Christianity in his kingdom and becoming a friend of influential churchmen. One of these friends was Benedict Biscop who was to benefit much from Cenwalh's generous gifts. Benedict was a Northumbrian scholar and founder of the twin monasteries of Monkwearmouth and Jarrow. He was a keen collector of books and

7

travelled far and wide over England and Europe to obtain precious manuscripts for his libraries. Another friend was Alchfrid, sub-king of Deira, part of the Northumbrian kingdom. Alchfrid was a keen supporter of the Roman branch of the Church and a close friend and admirer of Wilfrid, abbot of Ripon and bishop of York. The *Anglo-Saxon Chronicle* records Cenwalh's building of the old minster church at Winchester which seems to have been completed and consecrated in 648, the dedication being to St Peter. As Birinus did not die until 649 or 650 we may conclude that the church was dedicated by him.

It is not easy to assess the achievements of Bishop Birinus since there is so little known of him. The lack of detail in Bede's account of his character and activities has perhaps led to the assumption that his mission was ineffectual. Certainly Sir Frank Stenton attributes little success to his mission when he writes, "If an important member of the royal house, Cenwalh, delayed so long before accepting Christianity it is unlikely that Birinus secured any general conversion of the West Saxon people. The foundation of his church at Dorchester may well have been his principal achievement."*

Sir Frank Stenton's assessment of his mission is hardly in accord with Bede's statement that Birinus built and dedicated churches and brought many to the Lord by his holy labours. The initial refusal of King Cenwalh to accept Christianity cannot be regarded as a valid argument against the effectiveness of Birinus' mission. It is of interest to find that the sixth archbishop of Canterbury was a West Saxon by race. He was Deusdedit and, according to the *Anglo-Saxon Chronicle* was consecrated on 26th March 655. It is quite possible that Deusdedit had first learned the Faith from Bishop Birinus in his native Wessex, and had become one of his fellow clergy involved in the conversion of his own people. He was the first Englishman to become archbishop of Canterbury and must have been a man of learning and zeal to be selected for this high office. Bede also speaks of the priest, Wighard, as "one of Archbishop Deusdedit's clergy, a good man well fitted to be a bishop". It is not unlikely again that Deusdedit had brought Wighard with him from Wessex to assist him at Canterbury though there is no positive evidence for this. Wighard should have become archbishop after Deusdedit but the plague brought his life to a sudden end.

A number of local traditions and legendary tales are associated with the life and work of St Birinus. Churn Knob, an ancient burial

---

Anglo-Saxon England. F. Stenton.

site in Berkshire, observable from a great distance because of its elevated position, is alleged to have been the meeting place of Birinus and Cynigils. Here, too, it is said, the saint preached to the king. Berin's Hill, a one-time Roman military outpost, is believed to have been one of Birinus' favourite preaching places where he built himself a cell for his private devotions. These, and many other legends and traditions, are fully set out in J. E. Field's book, *St Berin, the Apostle of Wessex*. In his view the mission of Birinus to the West Saxons has never received the recognition which it deserves nor in proportion to the greatness of its results for, he says, "the royal house of Wessex, to which he brought the faith, was destined to become, two centuries later, the royal house of England."

CHAPTER TWO

Further Developments in Wessex

THE *F* manuscript of the *Anglo-Saxon Chronicle* records the death of Birinus and the consecration of his successor. The annal reads "650 — In this year Bishop Birinus passed away, and Agilbert the Frank was consecrated." Agilbert was to have a great influence not only on the Church in Wessex but on the English Church as a whole. He was a learned man and, before coming to Britain from his native Kingdom of the Franks, had gone to Ireland to study the Scriptures and remained there for some years.

Monasteries in Ireland were renowned for their learning and their well-stocked libraries. Their monks were generous in opening their doors to foreign students, charging them nothing for their food and instruction. Little wonder that students flocked to Ireland in droves, "like a swarm of bees," says Aldhelm, abbot of Malmesbury. Many, we may imagine, were there, less to satisfy their quest for knowledge than to enjoy a period of diversion from their every day activities. But Agilbert was a serious scholar and, in Ireland, extended his knowledge of biblical texts and other branches of religious study. Either here or in Gaul, where many Irish pilgrims and missionaries stayed, he acquired a knowledge of the beliefs and customs of the Celtic Church. Later he was a senior delegate at the important Council of Whitby which met to debate the differences in the usages of the Roman and Celtic Churches.

After leaving Ireland, Agilbert came to England, to the province of the West Saxons where Cenwalh was king. According to Bede, Agilbert was already a bishop when he arrived in England, and was therefore available to serve wherever there was a need in the English Church. Bede tells us that Agilbert came to the king, and, of his own accord, offered to evangelize Wessex.

Agilbert was welcomed by King Cenwalh and given freedom to preach to his people. Very soon Cenwalh, impressed by Agilbert's ability and enthusiasm, invited him to accept the vacant West Saxon see. Agilbert accepted and became the second bishop of the

West Saxons with his episcopal seat probably still at Dorchester-on-Thames. He held the bishopric for about ten or twelve years. It was during his episcopate that the West Saxon priest, Deusdedit, was consecrated archbishop of Canterbury.

According to the *Anglo-Saxon Chronicle* King Cenwalh was, from time to time, engaged in battles against both the Britons and the Mercians. In 652 he fought against the Britons at Bradford-on-Avon near Bath and in 658 at Penselwood, driving them westwards as far as the river Parret. To the north of his kingdom lay Mercia, now ruled by Penda's son, Wulfhere, a powerful warrior-king with ambition to expand his kingdom. In this he was successful, making himself master and overlord of Essex whose kings were subject to him. Through military victories Wulfhere also added parts of Cenwalh's kingdom of Wessex to his own Mercian kingdom. In 661 he ravaged the district of Ashdown in Berkshire and in the far south conquered the Isle of Wight which he gave to the king of Sussex, Ethelwalh.

Meanwhile the Church in Wessex advanced under the admininistration of Agilbert and the patronage of King Cenwalh. Discord, however, between king and bishop arose when the king appointed an additional bishop to work in Wessex, without having first consulted Agilbert. It was the kind of action on the part of a king which was to cause similar discord in the north some years later. Wilfrid was to protest vigorously against King Egfrid's appointment of other bishops to administer parts of his Northumbrian diocese without first gaining his approval. The King had acted over Wilfrid's head and usurped an authority which belonged to the Church. When Wilfrid found himself in this situation he must have recalled what had happened to his friend, Bishop Agilbert, some years before.

Apart from telling us that Cenwalh divided his kingdom into two sees, placing his new bishop, Wini, at Winchester, Bede explains that the king had grown increasingly irritated by Agilbert's foreign speech. He probably spoke a kind of pidgin English, a mixture of his own Frankish dialect and the Saxon tongue. It was understandable, but not easily so. His lack of fluency in Saxon is confirmed by a problem that arose at the Council of Whitby when Agilbert, because of his learning and seniority, should have been the chief spokesman for the Roman party. Rather than speak through interpreters he asked King Oswy, who was presiding over the council, to allow his disciple, Wilfred, to speak in his place, for "he can explain our view in the English language more competently and clearly than I . . . " King Cenwalh of Wessex must have found communication with Agilbert difficult. He wanted a bishop in his kingdom with whom he could exchange ideas freely. Such a man was Wini, an Englishman, who, like Wilfrid, had received episcopal ordination in Gaul.

If Cenwalh had intended that Bishop Agilbert should continue to work in his kingdom from his episcopal seat at Dorchester, Agilbert was to decide otherwise. Offended that he had not been consulted about the appointment of a second bishop, Agilbert resigned his bishopric in about 663, travelled north to be with his friends in Northumbria, and, no doubt, poured out his grievances to his young disciple, Wilfrid. It was while Agilbert was in Northumbria that he attended the Council of Whitby, defending the Roman position and appointing Wilfrid to be his spokesman. Wilfrid was then a priest and abbot of Ripon but Agilbert considered him worthy to become a bishop. Shortly after the Council of Whitby Agilbert returned to his native Gaul and became bishop of Paris, assisting soon after at the consecration of Wilfrid to the episcopate.

Cenwalh seems to have been no happier with his new bishop than he had been with the last. Wini was bishop for about three years only, possibly from 663 until 666 but the dates are not certain. Then, for a reason, which Bede either did not know or did not choose to disclose, Cenwalh drove him out of Wessex. Wini took refuge with King Wulfhere of Mercia. There was no episcopal vacancy in Mercia itself but Wulfhere agreed to sell the bishopric of London to Wini. Wini had apparently been infected by the corrupt practices of the Frankish Church where the sin of simony, the purchase of ecclesiastical gifts and preferment, was common.

Cenwalh was now without a bishop in his kingdom. The thought troubled him. Were the losses he was sustaining against his enemies due to his ill-treatment of his two bishops? Might not a kingdom without a bishop justly be deprived of God's protection? With these thoughts in mind Cenwalh sent envoys to Paris requesting the return of Agilbert to his bishopric of the West Saxons. But Agilbert replied that he could not return, since he was now responsible for his own bishopric in Paris. He had a nephew, however, who was a priest and worthy of the office of bishop. If the king agreed, he would send him to preach the faith in Wessex and to administer the diocese as its bishop. The king gladly accepted Agilbert's nephew, Leutherius, into his kingdom and sent him to Canterbury for episcopal ordination by Archbishop Theodore. The year was 670 and Leutherius was to govern the church in Wessex until 676 when he was succeeded by

Haeddi. Leutherius was among a number of bishops and clergy present at a council summoned by Theodore at Hertford in 672 to discuss various matters of ecclesiastical policy. Theodore was an able administrator and eager to see the English Church established on a disciplined basis of sound government and orthodox doctrine. Synods, it was decided, were to be held every year and large dioceses were to be divided to simplify organisation and to provide for the ever-growing number of converts. The West Saxon diocese was among those recommended for division though this did not take place until some years later. Leutherius no doubt returned to Wessex with reports of the business discussed at the synod and the decisions taken.

King Cenwalh lived for only about two years after the consecration of his new bishop. He died in 672 and after his death there seemed no obvious ruler to take his place. The *Anglo-Saxon Chronicle* records that for a year the kingdom was ruled by his queen, Sexburg. Bede tells us that for about ten years sub-kings seized power, dividing the kingdom up amongst themselves. But the *Chronicle* records the reign of a king, Centwini, during this period. The annal for the year 676 tells of the accession of Centwini, son of Cynigils, recording also that in 682 he drove the Britons towards the sea, probably westwards into Devonshire. Aldhelm, abbot of Malmesbury, speaks, too, of Centwini, his contemporary, as a powerful and successful king who ruled Wessex for many years. He could not have ruled, however, much beyond 685 for in that year we hear that Cadwalla began to contend for the kingdom. Further evidence for the reign of Centwini exists in the *Life of Wilfrid* by Eddius. He reports that when Wilfrid had been driven out of his northern bishopric by the king he took refuge in the court of the West Saxon, King Centwini. This was in the year 681.* Aldhelm also tells of King Centwini entering a monastery before his death. Perhaps he was driven there by Cadwalla, the next king to rule Wessex, whom Bede describes as "a young and vigorous prince of the Gewisse."

Cadwalla's reign was short, no longer than two or three years, yet in that time he came nearer than any other king since Caewlin to becoming overlord of the English. He appears first in Bede's *History* as a bloodthirsty young pagan intent upon restoring Wessex to the prominence it enjoyed under his great great-grandfather Ceawlin.

---

*Lives of the Saints. J. F. Webb (Penguin Classics).

Bede and the *Anglo-Saxon Chronicle* provide evidence of his military conquests and the extent of his territorial gains. In 686 "Cadwalla and Mull, his brother, laid waste Kent and the Isle of Wight." The Isle of Wight, as we have seen, belonged at this time to King Ethelwalh of Sussex who had received it as a gift from Wulfhere of Mercia. Cadwalla, wishing to regain this island, which once belonged to Wessex, made fierce attacks upon King Ethelwalh, killing him and laying waste his kingdom of Sussex, slaughtering his people and devastating his land, reducing those who survived to a state of slavery. His victorious army boarded ships, possibly at Portsmouth, and overran the Isle of Wight, killing many of its heathen inhabitants. Cadwalla planned to exterminate its entire population and to replace them with inhabitants from Wessex.

Cadwalla's conquest of the Isle of Wight cannot be seen in perspective without bringing Bishop Wilfrid into the picture. During the five years prior to its conquest by Cadwalla Bishop Wilfrid had been preaching the Gospel in Sussex under the patronage of King Ethelwalh, himself a baptised Christian. His mission to Sussex had been a successful and rewarding enterprise. He had made a pact of friendship with the king; he had taught its people the truths of the Faith and showed them ways to alleviate their hunger by catching fish from the sea; he had founded a monastery on an estate given to him by the king at Selsey. No attempt had yet been made by Wilfrid to evangelize the Isle of Wight. Though it was under the direct rule of King Ethelwalh of Sussex the island had its own king, named Arwald. Perhaps there were plans to evangelize the island, but the invasion of Sussex and Wight by Cadwalla and his brother, Mull, prevented it. According to Bede and Wilfrid's biographer, Eddius, the people of Wight were a savage and degenerate people, entirely heathen and ignorant of the name of Christ, having rejected an earlier preacher who had come to them.

Eddius gives a glowing account of the close ties of friendship between Wilfrid and his patron, King Ethelwalh of Sussex. If the account is genuine we would naturally conclude that Wilfrid was saddened by the death of Ethelwalh at the hands of the cruel pagan Cadwalla. Yet Eddius shows Wilfrid being a friend of both slayer and slain, victor and vanquished. He tells of the wonderful friendship between Wilfrid and Cadwalla. The latter made Wilfrid supreme counsellor over his kingdom of Wessex, honouring him with extensive lands and other gifts and promising that if Wilfrid would be his helper and spiritual father he would be to him an obedient son. Thus Eddius presents Wilfrid as beloved by both kings but omits the fact that one king killed the other. Bede is more realistic. He gives us a picture of Cadwalla as a ruthless and barbaric ruler intent upon expanding his territories at the expense of the slaughter of neighbouring tribes. Unlike Eddius, Bede says nothing of the close ties of friendship between Wilfrid and Cadwalla. He merely records that the king vowed to give a quarter of the Isle of Wight and its booty to the Lord if he should succeed in conquering it. The promise was fulfilled when, after his victory, he donated three hundred hides to Bishop Wilfrid, who then, with the help of the priest Hiddila, set about converting its pagan people.

Cadwalla had by now become master of the Isle of Wight and the kingdom of Sussex. His conquest of Sussex opened the way for the invasion of Kent. If we piece together the entry in the *Anglo-Saxon Chronicle* for the year 686, where we are told that Cadwalla and his brother Mull laid waste the kingdom of Kent, with a passage in Bede (*iv 26*) on the troubles of the Kentish line of succession at that time we can see the results of Cadwalla's expansionist policies. Yet even before Cadwalla's invasion of Kent it seems that there had been internal strife in that kingdom. Bede records the death of King Hlothere in February 685, as a result of the wounds he had sustained in a battle against Sussex, a battle which had been induced by his nephew, Edric. Edric then ruled the kingdom of Kent but for only about a year and a half. He died in the year 686, perhaps at the hands of Cadwalla of Wessex, who had begun his encroachments into Kentish territory. Bede then tells us that following Edric's death foreign kings and usurpers plundered the kingdom. These kings and usurpers must refer to Cadwalla and his brother Mull. The latter ruled the kingdom for a short time and a gruesome entry in the *Anglo-Saxon Chronicle* for the year 687 tells us what the men of Kent thought of him; "Mull was burnt to death in Kent and twelve other men with him." This act must have stirred Cadwalla to further attacks upon Kent which the *Anglo-Saxon Chronicle* records for the same year. Restitution was made six years later when the men of Kent paid Cadwalla's successor, King Ine, thirty thousand pence "because they had burnt Mul to death." Here we see an example of the Anglo-Saxon law of compensation, the payment of wergild to the offended party for the murder of someone belonging to their family; the wergild varied in amount according to the social status of the murdered man. In this case the wergild was high, since the murdered man was of royal blood.

After this period of turmoil in Kent, which lasted for about four years, the rightful king, Wictred, came to the throne and restored the kingdom to peace and prosperity, ruling it for thirty-four years, that is from about 690 or 691 to 725. He and his uncle Hlothere are of particular interest for the codes of law which they drew up for their people. Bede speaks of Wictred as a religious man and certainly there is a noticeably strong religious element in his code of laws.*

The character of Cadwalla, king of the West Saxons, is something of an enigma. We have seen him as an aggressive and daring young warlord, capable of savage acts of cruelty, a pagan who had not yet accepted the teaching of the Church, yet at the same time favourable to the Church and on good terms with the Christian preachers. A surviving charter shows him in 685-7 granting land at Farnham in the west of Surrey, over which he had gained authority, for the building of a monastery.

"I, Caedwalla, by the dispensation of the Lord, king of the Saxons, for the relief of my soul, confer on you, Cedde, Cisi and Criswa, into your possession for the construction of a monastery, the land whose name is Farnham, of 60 hides, of which 10 are in Binton, 2 in Churt . . . with everything belonging to them, fields, woods, meadows, pastures, fisheries, rivers, springs . . . Never at any time shall I and my heirs try to contravene this charter of donation."

Among the many signatures to the charter are those of Bishop Wilfrid, Bishop Earconwald of London, Bishop Haeddi of Winchester and Aldhelm, Abbot of Malmesbury.†

The *Anglo-Saxon Chronicle* records a further donation of land by Cadwalla to St Peter's monastery at Peterborough. The land, perhaps for the building of a daughter house though some distance from Peterborough, was at Hoo, between the estuaries of the Thames and Medway.

What is most surprising about Cadwalla is that at the height of his power when still a young man and when Wessex looked like becoming dominant among the kingdoms of the English he gave up everything, after a reign of only three years, and went off to Rome as a pilgrim to the shrines of St Peter and St Paul. The reason for this sudden abandonment of his political career may have been that

---

English Historical Documents. Vol. 1. No. 31

---

† *English Historical Documents*. Vol. 1. No. 58.

a new combination of circumstances had arisen. After a period of exile in his youth he had acquired power through force of arms and spent the rest of his short life immersed in war and bloodshed. During the fighting in the Isle of Wight he was wounded seriously enough to necessitate a period of quiet and seclusion to give the wounds time to heal. He witnessed the violent end of his brother Mull and twelve of his followers in Kent. Perhaps he had grown tired of a life of violence and craved a quieter existence. He was in all probability seriously ill, for we know that he died soon after reaching Rome.

His decision to become a pilgrim and to accept Christian baptism may have been the result of the influence of the devout churchmen with whom he was in contact. In his own kingdom was bishop Haeddi, successor to Leutherius. Bede describes him as "a good, just man, who carried out his duties as bishop guided by an inborn love of goodness rather than by anything learned from books." Miracles of healing were said to have occurred at the place of his death because of his great holiness. It was this Haeddi who was responsible for translating the body of Bishop Birinus from Dorchester-on-Thames to Winchester. Haeddi had his episcopal seat at Winchester which was also the royal seat of the kings of Wessex. It is possible that the young king's change of heart was partly due to the influence of his saintly bishop. There were other clerics, too, who must have left their mark upon Cadwalla: Earconwald, bishop of London, one of the signatories of the king's charter relating to the monastery at Farnham, was a man of outstanding virtue; Aldhelm, abbot of Malmesbury, renowned for his learning and wisdom, would certainly have been known to Cadwalla since he was a member of the royal house of Wessex; nor should we minimise the likely influence of Bishop Wilfrid who, as we have seen was made supreme counsellor over the whole kingdom. Wilfrid might have related to Cadwalla his experiences in Rome, how, as a young man, he visited the shrines of the saints and knelt before the pope to receive his blessing and how later he revisited the Holy City of Rome to make his appeal to the pope against his unlawful expulsion from the see of York.

In Bede's day renunciation of temporal power and worldly occupations for the purpose of making a pilgrimage to Rome was an act of spiritual merit. English kings, newly converted to the Faith, with paganism only a step behind them, followed the example of religious men and women, monks and nuns, priests and bishops, who made arduous journeys to Rome. Rome was not only the heart of the Christian world; there the two apostles, Peter and Paul, had lived and taught and died martyrs' deaths; and there, too, were the

Apostles' tombs where pilgrims went to pray. But King Cadwalla of the West Saxons wished for more than this. He had not yet received Christian baptism. Where better to receive it than at the shrine of the Apostles in Rome? He would wait then for baptism until he reached Rome, hoping to die soon after and to enter into eternal life.

His two wishes were fulfilled, for on Easter Saturday of 689 he was baptised in Rome and ten days later he died. His baptism took place in the presence of the pope, Sergius, who gave him the new name of Peter "that he might be linked by name to the most blessed Prince of the Apostles." Cadwalla was given a burial appropriate to a royal monarch in the church of St Peter in Rome. By the order of the pope, an epitaph, composed by the archbishop of Milan, was inscribed on his tomb. The epitaph tells how Cadwalla forsook his kingly crown, his wealth, possessions, kinsmen and noblemen and went on a pilgrimage to St Peter's shrine; how he laid aside his barbarous ways, received the name of Peter at his baptism and then, through heavenly grace, was received into the realms of light.

"Great the king's faith, Christ's mercy greater still,
Whose counsels far surpass all mortal skill.
From earth's remotest end, from Britain's Isle,
To Romulus' town o'er many a wearly mile,
Bearing his gifts by devious ways he passed
Until he gazed on Peter's shrine at last . . ."*

When an Anglo-Saxon king, like Cadwalla, resigned his crown to make a pilgrimage to Rome or to enter the cloister, as others did, there seemed no shortage of ambitious men of royal blood to take his place. Indeed one wonders whether pressure from these contenders for power sometimes precipitated an untimely resignation. But usually they resigned to become monks or pilgrims if they were too old or sick, or unsuited for kingly office, like King Sigbert of East Anglia who refused to bear arms and lead his warriors against the Mercian army. Bede, of course, ascribes to these royal monks and pilgrims motives of pure devotion, and such motives, in some cases, they may have had. But we may suspect that in other cases, what seems, on the surface, to have been a pious action, may have sprung from force of circumstances or outside pressure from political rivals.

---

*The Ecclesiastical History of the English People. Bede. Edited B. Colgrave and R. A. B. Mynors.

In the year 688 when Cadwalla left England for Rome a young prince of the royal house of Wessex, a great nephew of Cynigils, was the obvious successor to the throne. His name was Ine and he ruled the kingdom of the West Saxons from 688 to 726. Sir Frank Stenton calls him "the most important king of Wessex between Ceawlin and Egbert." We have, however, few details about his reign. Bede says little of him except that he ruled for thirty-seven years, then resigned in favour of younger men and went off to Rome as a pilgrim like his predecessor. A few entries in the *Anglo-Saxon Chronicle* relate to him. An insertion in the *A* manuscript tells that in 688 he built the monastery at Glastonbury, though it is more likely that he added finer buildings to those which already existed, for Glastonbury, as a religious centre, existed long before the time of Ine. William of Malmesbury, the twelfth century historian, tells us that it was Aldhelm, abbot of Malmesbury, who moved King Ine to build the monastery at Glastonbury. Another entry in the *Anglo-Saxon Chronicle* tells of his battles against Geraint, king of the Britons, in Cornwall in 710; and in 715 he was fighting against Ceolred of Mercia at Adams Grave in Alton Priors, Wiltshire. Sussex was kept under subjection by him, as it had been by Cadwalla, and the men of Kent came to terms with him and paid him a high sum to atone for their crime of having burnt Mull, the brother of Cadwalla.

Apart from his military and political power which established him as the strongest king in southern England, Ine was a loyal son of of the Church, concerned for the advancement of Christianity in his kingdom and statesmanlike in the practical steps he took to bring unity and cohesion to a somewhat fragmented West Saxon Church. In 705, under his inspiration, two sees were carved out of the one large see which had so far existed in Wessex. Winchester was retained as the episcopal seat of the eastern see, and in the west the new see of Sherborne was founded. Daniel was made bishop of Winchester and Aldhelm of Sherborne.

We have evidence from a contemporary *Life of Boniface* that King Ine initiated the holding of synods in Wessex. These were important since they allowed discussion to take place on matters of ecclesiastical policy. Decisions were taken, too, which settled local differences and brought agreement on Church affairs in Wessex. Wessex, of course, was not the first kingdom to introduce synods into its Church life. In 664 the Northumbrian Church convened the synod at Whitby, with King Oswy presiding, to discuss the Roman-Celtic question. In 672, Archbishop Theodore summoned a synod to be held at Hertford and he called a further synod at Hatfield in 680 to combat heresy and to reaffirm the true Faith regarding the nature of Christ. Theodore was still archbishop of Canterbury when Ine became king of Wessex in 688. We may surmise that both Theodore's policy of holding synods and of dividing large, unmanageable sees had their influence on Ine's policy within his own kingdom.

The account of the Wessex synod in *The Life of Boniface* shows that secular rulers were participants in the debates as well as religious leaders. King Ine was the instigator of the synod and he himself addressed the delegates.

"A sudden and urgent situation arose in the reign of Ine, King of the West Saxons . . . and immediately, by the counsel of the aforesaid king, a synodal council of the servants of God was held by the primates of the churches. And as soon as all were assembled, there took place among the priestly grades of the ecclesiastical order a most wholesome inquiry and deliberation about this recent dissention . . . And when this prudent discussion was concluded and all the council and the whole order of clerics assented, the king at once addressed all the servants of Christ . . . "*

We see here an example of the close association between the kings of early England and the bishops and clergy. There are, too, numerous examples of the presence of bishops at kings' councils, or witans, to discuss affairs of state.

According to the *Anglo-Saxon Chronicle*, King Ine's sister, Cuthberga, was the foundress of a double minster at Wimborne in Dorset. This would, presumably, have been founded with the support of Ine and on land donated by him. We have further evidence in a charter of Ine's granting land at Streatly-on-Thames and the surrounding district for the foundation of a monastery.

Ine's concern to safeguard the interests of the Church in Wessex is shown above all in his code of laws which have come down to us through King Alfred. Alfred had the laws copied as an addition to his own code and expressed his debt to them.

"Then I, King Alfred, collected these together and ordered to be written many of them which our forefathers observed, those

---

English Historical Documents. Vol. 1. No. 158

which I liked; and many of those which I did not like, I rejected with the advice of my councillors, and ordered them to be differently observed . . . But those which I found anywhere, which seemed to me most just, either of the time of my kinsman, King Ine, or of Offa, king of the Mercians, or of Ethelbert, who first among the English received baptism, I collected herein and omitted others."*

The laws of King Ine, as we have them, number seventy-six but as Professor Whitelock has pointed out, "It is not safe to assume that we have them complete, for King Alfred may have had copied only such as were useful for his purpose, and have ignored any which time had made a dead letter." Indeed, there are laws in the code of his contemporary, King Wictred of Kent, such as those against pagan practices, which we might have thought would appear in Ine's code. One of the laws in Ine's code is almost identical to one in Wictred's and relates to the necessity for a foreigner, when entering alien territory, to shout or blow a horn to prove his innocence and to warn of his presence there. The appearance of this law in both codes has led to the speculation that there may have been some collaboration between the two kings.

A comparison between Ine's code of laws, compiled some time around 694, and the earliest Kentish code belonging to King Ethelbert, compiled at the beginning of the century, reveals how Anglo-Saxon society had advanced in the intervening years. It had become much more complex and organised by the end of the century. Ethelbert's primitive code, compiled when he and his people were only a step away from their pagan past, reads like a catalogue of penalties and compensations to be paid for injuries, some very trivial, against one's neighbour. Ine's code, on the other hand, covers the whole spectrum of a well organised agricultural society, omitting the trivial and dealing with the basic and important aspects of a multifarious society. Like the Kentish code of Wictred, it reflects, too, the all pervasive influence of Christianity and its impact on culture, while at the same time, Anglo-Saxon society retained its distinctive Germanic character.

Ine, in the Prologue to his code, lists those who had assisted him in its compilation. They comprised both religious and secular persons who, by their diversity of outlook, contributed to the comprehensiveness of the code. They included Ine's father Cenred,

---

*The Laws of Ine. English Historical Documents. Vol. 1. No. 32.

named first in the list and most likely, his chief adviser; Haeddi, his own bishop of the West Saxons who had held office for almost twenty years and was a man of innate wisdom and virtue; Earconwald, bishop of London, to whom Ine refers as "my bishop", showing West Saxon ascendancy at that time over the East Saxons of Essex; his earldormen and chief councillors and "also a great assembly of the servants of God". The laws, he says, had been drawn up as a result of an enquiry "about the salvation of our souls and the security of our kingdom, that true law and true statutes might be established and strengthened throughout our people."

Although the law code covers many aspects of a farming community's life and legislates on such matters as murder, theft, marriage contracts, slavery, fencing of homesteads, felling of trees, straying of cattle and swine, there are many which relate specifically to the Church.

2. A child is to be baptized within 30 days; if it is not, 30 shillings compensation is to be paid.

3. If a slave works on Sunday at his master's command, he is to be free, and the master is to pay 30 shillings as a fine.

4. Church-scot is to be given by Martinmas; if anyone does not discharge it, he is to be liable to 60 shillings fine and to render the church-scot twelve fold.

5. If anyone is liable to the death penalty and he reaches a church, he is to retain his life and to compensate as the law directs him.

6. If anyone fights in a minster, he is to pay 120 shillings compensation.

45. Forcible entry into the residence of the king or bishop, within his own diocese, one shall compensate with 120 shillings.

The last we hear of King Ine in the pages of Bede is of his pilgrimage to Rome to the shrines of the Apostles where he wished to spend some of the time left to him, hoping, thereby, to merit a joyous welcome from the saints in heaven. The *Anglo-Saxon Chronicle*, too, records his pilgrimage: "726. In this year Ine went to Rome, and Aethelheard, his kinsman, succeeded to the kingdom of Wessex and ruled fourteen years."

In this chapter I have tried to give an outline of the historical and religious background of Wessex, against which we can now view the outstanding ecclesiastical figures of the kingdom in seventh and early eighth century England. We have seen how the Faith was first brought to Wessex by Bishop Birinus. We turn now to Aldhelm, monk and scholar of Malmesbury, second only to Bede in the extent of his learning and in the influence he had upon contemporary and later scholars, writers, churchmen and others. Apart from the vast difference in their literary styles, Bede's clear and unadorned, Aldhelm's artificial and obscure, another difference between the two men lay in the type of work they were involved in within the Church. Bede's work was entirely in the field of learning, Aldhelm's mainly in administration, first as abbot of Malmesbury and then as bishop of Sherborne. His literary output might well have equalled Bede's had he not been involved in these more practical affairs. But the obscurity of his style would never have won for him the attention and devotion of scholars which, for centuries Bede's work has done.

CHAPTER THREE

St Aldhelm, Abbot of Malmesbury and Bishop of Sherborne

OUR knowledge of Aldhelm is derived chiefly from a short account given by his young contemporary, Bede, in his *Ecclesiastical History*, and from the *Life of Aldhelm* by the twelfth century historian, William of Malmesbury. The latter was a monk of Malmesbury writing some four hundred years or so after Aldhelm's death but with access to original documents and letters relating to his life and the early history of the monastery. He was the librarian at Malmesbury, a visitor to other monasteries and libraries and an avid reader and collector of books. His best known writings are his *History of Kings* and *History of Prelates*. In Book Five of the latter is his *Life of Aldhelm*.

Aldhelm was born in about 639 when King Cynigils was ruling the West Saxon kingdom. He was of royal blood, though his precise connection with the royal house of Wessex is not known. At the time he was born, the missionary bishop, Birinus, had been preaching in the kingdom for several years. Aldhelm was about eleven when Birinus died in 650, so might well have remembered something of his mission to the West Saxons.

Birinus, as we have seen, belonged to the Roman Church and had come to Britain under papal authority. At his episcopal seat, Dorchester-on-Thames, he no doubt formed a religious community of fellow monks, oblates and laybrothers who received instruction in the Scriptures, the observance of a monastic rule and other aspects of religious life. Yet it was not the monastery and school associated with Birinus which acquired fame as a place of learning in Wessex. It was the Celtic monastery at Malmesbury, founded by an Irish monk, Maelduib, which became the most important centre of learning in the West Saxon kingdom. More than that, it was the most important in the whole of southern England until it was eclipsed by Theodore's school at Canterbury. It was to Maelduib's monastery at Malmesbury that Aldhelm, as a boy of about fifteen, was sent.

The monastery had been founded in about 635. Maelduib belonged to that class of Irishman who left their native land to become pilgrims for Christ and to undertake work in His name. Maelduib's wanderings brought him to the kingdom of the West Saxons, close to the forest of Selwood where he built himself a hermit's hut. Here, as an anchorite, he spent his time in prayer and study and the various forms of ascetic exercise so beloved of the Celtic monks. Soon, like other hermits of the desert, he attracted disciples in search of knowledge and spiritual counsel. To those who came he gave instruction in the Faith, imparting to them the skills of reading and writing, opening their eyes to the mysteries of the Scriptures, expounding to them the doctrines of the Church. Those who wished to learn more from him built themselves rough dwellings around his hermitage and began to follow the Rule which he himself observed and taught. So the monastery grew and as the number of his disciples increased so more buildings were needed: individual cells for the monks, a kitchen, refectory, infirmary, and a church for celebration of the Mass and the reciting of the daily Offices.

By the time Aldhelm entered the monastery in about 654 it had existed for twenty or so years and had gained a reputation for scholarship and religious devotion. The small collection of books which Maelduib had been able to bring with him in the early years of his pilgrimage had now multiplied. Books were rare and precious in Maelduib's day, every one being meticulously copied by hand. The Irish schools in particular were famous for their skill in copying and illuminating manuscripts and scribes were continually at work in the scriptoria of the monasteries making copies of the Scriptures, the Lives of the Saints, Church Histories and so on. During his years as abbot of the monastery, Maelduib most likely returned to Ireland from time to time to obtain more books for his library. Books were often borrowed from other libraries for transcription, some were bought from merchants from overseas, and keen collectors, like Benedict Biscop, founder of the monastery at Monkwearmouth, travelled to Italy and Gaul to obtain books on a wide range of subjects.

Accomplished Latin scholars like Aldhelm studied with ease the varied works of famous writers. Among these would have been the writings of the Apostolic Fathers and the four Latin Doctors of the Church, Ambrose, Augustine, Gregory and Jerome. A study of the Scriptures with commentaries took pride of place in the monks' curriculum, but many other religious works were studied, such as the Lives of the Saints, Church Histories, Christine Doctrine, a

25

study of the great Monastic Rules of the past, Prayers, Penitentials and Religious Verse. Then there were the more secular branches of study to engage the scholar's attention: Grammar, Rhetoric and Dialectic, Poetry and Versification, Music and Chant, Arithmetic, Astronomy and Geometry.

In 661 when Aldhelm was about twenty-two he took monastic vows and received the tonsure from the abbot, Maelduib. If Maelduib had come from southern Ireland, where many clergy had adopted Roman customs long before the Synod of Whitby of 664, his monastery at Malmesbury by now most likely conformed to the pattern of Rome in its Easter celebrations and the form of tonsure worn by its monks with the crown of the head shaven. If however Maelduib had come from the north of Ireland, which was slower and more reluctant to accept the usages of Rome, it is likely that, in its early years, his monastery was governed on Celtic lines. After the Synod of Whitby, however, when the English Church decided in favour of Rome, Malmesbury, like other Celtic monasteries, would have changed its customs to conform to those of Rome.

Except for two terms of study at Canterbury, four years at Sherborne and a visit to Rome, Aldhelm was to stay at Malmesbury for the rest of his life. In 671, in his early thirties, he went to the famous school at Canterbury to study under Hadrian and Theodore. The school was attached to the monastery of St Peter and St Paul of which Hadrian was abbot. Hadrian is described by Bede as "very learned in the Scriptures, experienced in ecclesiastical and monastic administration and a great scholar in Greek and Latin." Theodore had recently been appointed to the archbishopric of Canterbury and of him Bede says "he was learned both in sacred and secular literature, in Greek and Latin and of proved integrity." Because of their learning these men attracted students from far and wide. Great numbers came to Canterbury and were instructed in the Scriptures, music, poetry, astronomy and the calculation of the Church's calendar. "Never had there been such happy times as these," says Bede, "since the English settled in Britain."

The Canterbury school offered to gifted students, like Aldhelm, not only a high level of teaching but contact with other first class minds. A number of students who had studied under Theodore and Hadrian were alive in Bede's day; many, he says, were as proficient in Greek and Latin as they were in their own native language. He names a few of such men who either studied or taught at Canterbury. Benedict Biscop had close connections with the monastery at Canterbury and based the organisation and government of his own monastery at Monkwearmouth on that of Canterbury. Oftfor, before being made bishop of Worcester had studied in the two monasteries of St Hilda at Hartlepool and Whitby, followed by a period of study in Canterbury. John, bishop of Beverley and Hexham, had studied under Theodore and once recalled how Theodore had warned of the danger of blood-letting at the time of the full moon. Tobias, bishop of Rochester, is described by Bede as "a learned man who had been a disciple of Archbishop Theodore and Abbot Hadrian." Albinus, who was to succeed Hadrian as abbot of the monastery at Canterbury, had been educated under the two scholars, and was to acquire such a complete command of Latin that he could speak it as fluently as his native Saxon.

So absorbed was Aldhelm in his studies at Canterbury during his second visit that in a letter to his friend Leutherius, bishop of the West Saxons, who had ordained him to the priesthood, he says he regrets that he must let Christmas pass without returning to Malmesbury to join the brethren. His mind, he says, is preoccupied with the study of Roman Law, music, arithmetic and astrology and a hundred different kinds of poetic metre. There is so much to learn and so little time in which to learn it.*

In 675 Aldhelm wrote a letter to Abbot Hadrian expressing a wish to return to Canterbury once more, but he says he has been prevented from doing so because of sickness; "since I was cut off from residence in your friendly society on my departure from Kent about three years ago I have burned with the ardent desire to be with you again; and I have long intended to carry out this desire, if change and circumstances allowed and various obstacles did not come in the way; especially if I were not prevented by bodily weakness through an affliction which parches to the marrow my wasting limbs; this it was that when, after my first course, I was with you again, drove me home."

In about 675, at the age of thirty-six, Aldhelm was elected abbot of the monastery at Malmesbury, in place of Maelduib who had recently died. He remained abbot until his death in 709 and was, during the last four years of his life, also bishop of Sherborne. As abbot he ruled the monastery with wisdom and devotion, teaching in the school and imparting to his students the treasures of

---

*For an interesting suggestion that Aldhelm's legal studies in Canterbury may have resulted in his having a hand in drafting King Ine's code of laws, see *The Coming of Christianity to Anglo-Saxon England*. H. Mayr-Harting.

knowledge he had stored up in his mind over the years. As in most English monasteries at the time the Rule of St Benedict was taught and followed at Malmesbury, supplemented by extracts from other well-known rules.

One of Aldhelm's first tasks as abbot of Malmesbury was to replace Maelduib's simple church, probably built mainly of timber, with a larger and finer church of stone. The last quarter of the seventh century was an age of builders. Wilfrid in the north, whom Aldhelm befriended and supported against his enemies, was building splendid churches at Ripon and Hexham, the latter "supported by columns of various styles and with numerous side aisles, the walls of remarkable height and length, the many winding passages and spiral staircases leading up and down . . . a superb edifice with splendid gold and silver ornaments." No such description survives of Aldhelm's church at Malmesbury but we may imagine that it was one of considerable size and splendour. When the building was complete, Aldhelm composed a poem of twenty-one lines to mark the occasion of its dedication to the Saints Peter and Paul.

A story is told in *King Alfred's Handbook* of how Aldhelm, distressed by the practice of some churchgoers of slipping out of church when the time of the sermon arrived, won the attention of his flock by standing on the bridge over which they must pass on their way home and posing as a minstrel. Drawing on his knowledge of verse and song he would delight his audience with songs and the sweet sounds of his harp. When he had won their attention he would forsake these little compositions of secular verse and begin to sing on religious themes and to speak of God. Of his poetic compositions Charles Plummer has commented, "How willingly would we surrender the whole of Aldhelm's stilted Latin to recover one of his native poems!" Aldhelm must have been a poet of great talent, a number of his lays were still being sung, over two hundred years later, in Alfred's time and considered by Alfred to be "superior to all other English poetry."*

During his years as abbot of Malmesbury Aldhelm received many endowments of land for the enrichment of his monastery and for the establishment of daughter houses in various parts of Wessex. King Centwini, he says, was one such benefactor, making grants of land to him and generous gifts for the abbey at Glastonbury. Mercian kings also made grants of land to Aldhelm. King Ethelred is

---

Venerabilis Baedae. Charles Plummer. P. 309

associated with the foundation of the monastery at Abingdon, a few miles south west of Dorchester-on-Thames which had come under Mercian domination through military victory. This same Mercian king gave land to Aldhelm at Tetbury in south Gloucestershire and at Long Newton in north Wiltshire. In 685 he received a large estate of forty hides at Somerford Keynes, south of Cirencester, from Ethelred's nephew, Ethelred himself confirming the gift. The estate was to help to support the monks of Malmesbury.*

In addition to the church at Malmesbury built by Aldhelm to replace Maelduib's simple structure, he built two others. One was dedicated to Mary, the Mother of God, the other to St Michael the Archangel. The latter was still standing, or partly so, in William of Malmesbury's time in the twelfth century. He describes it as excelling in size and beauty any ancient church in England.

Aldhelm founded other religious houses not far from Malmesbury. These were at Bradford-on-Avon, the church dedicated, as it is today to St Lawrence, and, though mainly tenth century, containing some much older stonework probably from Aldhelm's time. The other was at Frome in Somerset, dedicated to St John the Baptist.

Wareham, north of Corfe Castle, in Dorset, is associated with another of Aldhelm's foundations. Like the present partly pre-conquest church at Wareham, Aldhelm's church was dedicated to St Martin, a favourite saint in early Anglo-Saxon times. Tradition claims that Aldhelm's church at Wareham was begun while he waited in the district for a favourable wind to take him by ship across the Channel. On this occasion he was bound for Rome. In William of Malmesbury's day the church was still standing but had no roof. Local peasants and wayfarers often resorted to it for shelter against the rain, for it was claimed that, even though the building was roofless, it never let the rain fall within its stout walls. The spirit of Aldhelm watched over it, they said, and all attempts to reroof it failed. So the miracle of its imperviousness to the rain was perpetuated and pilgrims came there in their thousands on Saint Aldhelm's Day. They came too on pilgrimages to Malmesbury where Aldhelm's body was enshrined.

We may wonder whether Aldhelm had any connection with the headland, named after him, to the west of Swanage. On St Aldhelm's Head there is a small twelfth century chapel, St Aldhelm's

---

*Anglo-Saxon England. F. Stenton. P. 151

chapel. Perhaps this marks the site of an earlier chapel or cell built by him or his predecessor, Maelduib. The site is typical of those chosen by Celtic monks for their hermitages, with expansive views of sea and sky.

William of Malmesbury tells us that Aldhelm, having completed his task of building churches and daughter houses of Malmesbury abbey, wished to visit Rome to obtain from Pope Sergius a letter of privilege safeguarding his monastery and its estates against interference from future bishops of Wessex. In the north of England, Ceolfrith, abbot of the twin monasteries of Montwearmouth and Jarrow, was also to do the same, sending envoys to Pope Sergius to obtain letters of privilege for his monasteries. Apart from this practical reasons for going to Rome, Aldhelm must have cherished a desire to visit the shrines of the Apostles Peter and Paul, as so many others were doing at the time, including his friend Wilfrid, and the young King Cadwalla. Ine, too, was to end his days in Rome. It was to King Ine that Aldhelm confided his wish to visit Rome and from him he received approval. King Ethelred of Mercia, another of Aldhelm's patrons and benefactors, was also consulted and gave his support to the proposal.

In Rome Aldhelm was given hospitality in the Lateran Palace and every day celebrated Mass. William of Malmesbury, describing this episode in Aldhelm's life, says that the chasuble he wore in Rome was still preserved in the abbey at Malmesbury. William described it as of most delicate material, dyed scarlet, with scroll designs, in black, containing representations of peacocks. Aldhelm obtained the charter of privilege from Pope Sergius which granted to the monasteries of Malmesbury and Frome exemption from episcopal jurisdiction. No cleric, whatever his status, was permitted to say Mass in the monastic churches except by invitation of the abbot. When the abbot died, the monks were to elect a successor. Aldhelm returned to England with the charter which was then signed by Ine, king of Wessex, and Ethelred, king of Mercia, both kings agreeing that, though strife might break out between the two kingdoms, the monasteries should be left in peace.

During his early years as a monk at Malmesbury, and less so as abbot of the monastery, Aldhelm devoted much time to study and writing. From the works that have come down to us it is evident that he was a man of deep learning, familiar with the writings of the Spanish author and bishop, Isidore of Seville, and his encyclopaedic work *Etymologies*. He was familiar too with classical writers such as Cicero, Ovid, Pliny, Virgil and the poet and writer of riddles,

Symphosius. As an English scholar and writer Aldhelm pre-dates Bede. He claims to be the first of his race to turn his mind to the study of Latin verse and metre. Bede describes Aldhelm's literary style as lucid. Could he really have meant it? Later scholars have described it as pompous, obscure, artificial and involved. Even in English translation it is all of these. It seems that he had been influenced by a style of writing popularised by Irish scholars which made use of abstruse and strange sounding words derived from Greek, Hebrew and other sources and arranged in lengthy and complicated sentences. It is a style as intricate and bewildering as are the artistic designs of Celtic art with their endless linear convolutions. Perhaps he had learned the style from his teachers at Maelduib's Irish monastery at Malmesbury.*

Among Aldhelm's writings that lie tucked away and largely unread in academic libraries there is a dissertation on poetic metre and another on the mystical meaning of the number seven, a treatise in prose and verse on virginity, a hundred riddles, religious poems and letters. Of his vernacular verse which he set to music and sang for his wayward parishioners nothing survives. Perhaps he had heard of the Northumbrian poet, Caedmon, who also composed religious verse, for the edification and instruction of the local population of Whitby. Caedmon, a simple cowherd, who could neither read nor write, had received the gift of poetry direct from heaven after which he captivated his listeners with the beauty and wisdom of his verse.

Aldhelm's work on poetic metre, together with his study of the mystical meaning of the number seven and his hundred riddles, were sent to his friend, King Aldfrid of Northumbria who ruled from 685 to 705. He had been a pupil with Aldhelm at Malmesbury and shared Aldhelm's love of books and learning. Aldfrid was connected with the royal house of Wessex through his marriage to King Ine's sister, Cuthberga. But either at the start of the marriage or some time later Cuthberga had left her husband to enter the double monastery at Barking in Essex. We may wonder whether Aldhelm encouraged her decision to enter the cloister. Cuthberga, as the wife of his friend King Aldfrid, and as the sister of King Ine, must have been well known to Aldhelm. We hope that he did not encourage

---

*For an alternative theory that Aldhelm's style was derived from continental writers, see *Anglo-Saxon England* (6). Edited P. Clemoes and *Aldhelm's Prose style and its Origins* by M. Winterbottom.

Cuthberga to enter the cloister against the wishes of her husband in the same way as Wilfrid had done with the wife of King Egfrid. Egfrid had married Etheldreda, who also yearned to enter the cloister and Wilfrid had encouraged it. This added to Egfrid's already hostile relations towards Wilfrid, since in this matter he had expected him to support his wish to keep Etheldreda as his wife and queen.

Aldhelm's lengthy treatise *In Praise of Virginity* was not addressed to Cuthberga in particular. It was addressed to Hildilid, the abbess of Barking and her nuns, of whom Cuthberga was one, and she may well have been uppermost in his mind when he composed the work. In it he exalts the celibate life above that of marriage. It is like gold to silver, he says, like silk to wool. Marriage, of course, is not to be despised; this would be contrary to the Faith of the Church. "Indeed the glory of virginity has grown out of the law of wedlock, just as gold comes from the earth, the rose from the thorn, the pearl from the shell." There is a difference between the wife and the virgin. The wife, says Aldhelm, busies herself in "delicate arrangements, the hair twisted into curls with the iron, the cheeks and jaws coloured with red antimony, like those of swine. The virgin with hair unkempt and careless, will carry the palm of chastity and wear on her head the crown of glory."*

The nuns of Barking were evidently women of intellect as well as piety. Aldhelm in his treatise refers to the studies in which they were engaged: the Old and New Testaments, commentaries and allegorical interpretation of the Scriptures, the science of time, a study of words, grammar and metre. For all these studies a thorough knowledge of Latin was necessary since this was the language of scholarship. It must have been no mean intellectual feat on the part of the nuns to understand the treatise he had sent them, written in his customary obscure and artificial style. In his efforts to encourage the nuns in the celibate life he draws upon a variety of sources, from the writings of Ambrose, Augustine, Cassian, Cyprian and Tertullina, from the Bible and from stories of monks and nuns, saints and martyrs. The work, he tells them, was written in stages when time allowed. He ends thus, "Forgive the faults of this letter, put together, bit by bit, among the distractions of a busy life, in fear and peril of error . . . May your prayers rise to aid and support me in my labours; for truly I myself struggle among the waves of my own

Anglo-Saxon Saints and Scholars. E. Duckett

faults, while I strive to guide others toward the shore of perfection. And so farewell, flowers of the Church, sisters of the convent, disciples of learning, pearls of Christ, jewels of Paradise and heirs of our home-to-be in Heaven."*

In his letter to King Aldfrid, Aldhelm again complains of being weighed down with religious affairs. As abbot of Malmesbury he would have been responsible for attending to the administration of the monastery and the management of its estates, with control also of the daughter houses at Bradford-on-Avon and Frome. Much of the teaching too, at Malmesbury must have been done by him, on account of his wide learning. Then there was spiritual counselling to be given, letters to be written, visiting to be done, and, most important of all, the daily Offices to be said with other monks in the monastic church. Priority was given, too, to his private prayers and hours of reading for, said he, "when I read, I listen to God speaking, and when I pray I speak to God." Into this busy, active life, Aldhelm managed to find time to write his many letters, poems, riddles and treatises.

The work sent to King Aldfrid of Northumbria falls into four parts. First comes a study of the use of the number seven in the Old and New Testaments and in the world of nature. The study is introduced by a reminder to Aldfrid, "most excellent and best-loved son" of their friendship at the time when he, Aldfrid, received the sevenfold gift of the Spirit in Confirmation. Second comes a treatise on the different kinds of poetic metre and their use in literature. Third there is a remarkable piece of creative writing in the form of a hundred riddles in verse form. Fourth comes a study of the rules of poetic feet. The riddles illustrate a type of literature popular among the Anglo-Saxons. Aldhelm's riddles were written in Latin and modelled on those of a fifth century writer, Symphosius. They vary in length, from four lines to eighty-three. The reader will have no difficulty discovering the answer to this riddle.

"On high and rocky shore, lashed by dark sea,
Where breakers swell upon the ocean's plain,
Man's craft has raised my tower of massive stone
That I may point safe pathways to their ships.
Not mine to traverse ocean fields,
Nor plough the sea in boats with winding course!
Yet, as they labour, driven among the waves,

---

*Anglo-Saxon Saints and Scholars. E. Duckett

From my high watch I lead these ships to shore,
Setting within my tower a torch aloft
When clouds and fog blot out the flame of stars."*

By the time Aldhelm had reached the age of about sixty-six plans were going ahead for the division of the large West Saxon diocese. Theodore, archbishop of Canterbury until the year 690, had pioneered the policy of dividing large dioceses in various parts of the country, thereby easing the burden of existing bishops and also providing extra ones to minister to the ever-growing number of Christian converts in England. The sees of East Anglia and Northumbria had been divided, under the initiative of Theodore. Now his successor, Bertwald, continued the same policy. In 705, after the death of the West Saxon bishop, Haeddi, a council of bishops, with the support of King Ine, was held to discuss the state of the Church in Wessex. Agreement was reached that the see should be divided to form two separate dioceses, each with its own bishop. The eastern diocese was to be administered by Bishop Daniel, with his episcopal seat at Winchester. The diocese to the west of Selwood was to be administered by Aldhelm, his seat at Sherborne. The appointment of Aldhelm to Sherborne was a wise one, for he knew the area well, having spent fifty or so years at Malmesbury, keeping in close touch, too, with the daughter houses at Bradford-on-Avon, Frome and possibly others. He would, moreover, have as his western neighbour the kingdom of the British in Devon and Cornwall with the opportunity of influencing them in the acceptance of the universal customs of the Roman Church. Shortly before his appointment to Sherborne, Aldhelm had, because of his erudition, been chosen to write a letter of admonition to the king of the British, Geraint, urging him and the British clergy to fall into line with the Roman Church and to adopt their Easter customs and their form of tonsure.

Like the saintly Cuthbert of Northumbria, Aldhelm resisted appointment to a bishopric, his resistance enhancing, in the eyes of his contemporaries and future admirers, his humility. Aldhelm was no ecclesiastical climber. He wished to end his days quietly at Malmesbury, in the monastery so dear to him, where he could pray, study and write and continue to teach the younger brethren. He protested that he was too old for a bishopric, but the council

---

Anglo-Saxon Saints and Scholars. E. Duckett

rejected his protest saying that maturity brought with it greater wisdom and freedom from vices. Aldhelm at last relented, not wishing to oppose the voice of God. So the appointment was made and Aldhelm became a colleague to the other bishops, a father to the clergy and a protector of the laity.

In the autumn of 705 he went to Canterbury to be consecrated bishop, by Archbishop Bertwald, who shared with him a knowledge of monastic life. Before becoming archbishop, Bertwald had been abbot of a community of monks at Reculver on the north coast of Kent. Bede said of him "he was a man with a deep knowledge of the Scriptures and well versed in ecclesiastical and monastic teaching, but not to be compared with his predecessor."

Aldhelm welcomed a return to Canterbury. It reminded him of his early days when he had studied under Theodore and Hadrian, the latter still being alive at the time of his present visit. Aldhelm stayed in Canterbury as long as time would allow. He did not miss the opportunity of visiting the port of Dover where ships came in from the Continent laden with all kinds of merchandise. Among some manuscripts he found a complete copy of the Old and New Testaments for which he offered the mariners a price. But they, thinking it was too low, jeered at him and drove him from their ship and put out to sea again. Soon after, a storm arose, waves dashed against their ship, putting their lives in jeopardy. In fear they stretched out their arms to the man of God who prayed for their deliverance. At once the storm abated and the mariners drew in to land again. "The book is yours Sir! We will accept no payment," said the men. But Aldhelm insisted on giving them a fair price for the manuscript which he took back with him to Canterbury and from thence to Malmesbury. William of Malmesbury, over four hundred years later, declared that it was still in the library of the monastery and that it was examined with interest by many pilgrims and travellers.

William tells us little about Aldhelm's four years as bishop of Sherborne. He preached day and night, he says, diligently travelling to various parts of the diocese, observing fasts as in his youth and giving himself to good works. Bede remarks that he administered the see energetically. In Sherborne he built a fine church, its foundations thought to be under the nave of the present medieval church. In addition to his episcopal duties he continued as abbot of the monastery at Malmesbury, the monks refusing to elect another abbot while Aldhelm still lived. He had control too of the two daughter foundations at Bradford-on-Avon and Frome. It may have been through his initiative or through the inspiration he implanted in others that many more monastic communities were founded in Wessex. This part of England is remarkable for the number of places with the suffix *minster*, to their names, as, for instance, in Axminster, Iwerne Minster, Sturminster, Warminster and Yetminster.

In 709, at the age of about seventy, Aldhelm was taken ill while on a visit to the village of Doulting, two miles east of Shepton Mallet in Somerset. He asked to be carried into the simple timber church in the village and there, soon after, he died. At that selfsame hour his friend, Egwin, bishop of Worcester in Mercia, had a strange presentiment that Aldhelm had died. William of Malmesbury goes further and says it was revealed to him in a vision that Aldhelm lay dead at Doulting, Egwin himself being commanded to go at once to the place. Straight away Egwin rode southwards, stopping no doubt for a short visit to the monks of Malmesbury. The journey to Doulting, being a distance of some eighty to a hundred miles, must have taken him some days to complete on horseback. In Doulting church Egwin said a Requiem Mass for his departed friend and later arranged for his body to be taken to Malmesbury where Aldhelm had wished to be buried.

As the funeral procession passed through towns and villages, crowds came to watch or to follow the bier, pushing their way forward to be as near to it as possible. Every seven miles of the fifty mile journey from Doulting to Malmesbury the procession stopped for rest and at every stopping place a stone cross was erected to commemorate the different stages of the journey. Later these crosses became known as "Bishopstones" and were still to be seen in William's day, one in the monks' cloister at Malmesbury. On reaching Malmesbury, Aldhelm's body was laid to rest in the church of St Michael, the monks lamenting the loss of their abbot and father.

For about two centuries the body remained in the church. Then, in 955, it was exhumed and transferred to a marvellous shrine, given some years before by King Ethelwulf, father of Alfred the Great. The shrine was beautifully adorned with silver, showing representations of the miracles which Aldhelm was said to have performed. The shrine became a place of pilgrimage in succeeding years, its most illustrious pilgrim the handsome and noble King Athelstan, grandson of Alfred the Great. Athelstan became a great benefactor of the town and abbey of Malmesbury, Aldhelm being his favourite saint and one to whom he prayed before the battle of Brunanburh. He too was buried in the abbey church and there today, carved by craftsmen of the middle ages, stands a splendid effigy of the king.

In the tenth century, Dunstan, the great religious reformer, abbot of Glastonbury and archbishop of Canterbury, gave bells of rich and resonant tone to Malmesbury Abbey and an organ on which were inscribed the words "I, Dunstan, Chief Bishop, gave this organ to Aldhelm." Lanfranc, a later archbishop of Canterbury (1070-1089), hearing of the miracles that had been wrought at the shrine in Malmesbury declared that throughout the English realm Aldhelm was to be known as Saint Aldhelm and to have his place in the Calendar of Saints. Thereafter this monk of Malmesbury and bishop of Sherborne was known as St Aldhelm, his feast day 25th May.

In the twelfth century the abbey church was rebuilt in Romanesque style, far grander than had been the smaller Saxon church. The library was founded and its fame became known throughout Europe, its most renowned librarian and historian being William of Malmesbury. The thirteenth century saw a further enlargement of the church and the addition of more domestic buildings for the monks' quarters. In the next century the church must have been at its finest with a lantern tower in the centre surmounted by a spire reputed to be taller than that of Salisbury Cathedral. But the architects and builders had been too clever and the tower and spire fell crashing to the ground in the middle of the sixteenth century. Malmesbury church today, splendid as it is, is only a fraction of the size it once was. When the monasteries were dissolved by Henry VIII, the church was sold to a rich cloth merchant, William Stumpe, who subsequently donated it to the people of Malmesbury for a parish church, and that is what it is today. So the visitor, as he stands in the glorious nave, or worships with the congregation, can call to mind that the worship of God has continued in this place since the Irish monk, Maelduib, in the seventh century, came to spread the Faith among the heathen West Saxons. To remind one also that for centuries Malmesbury was a centre of monastic life, there remains in the town today a small convent of nuns of the Order of St Andrew. They reside in the ancient Abbey House and there recite their daily offices. They assist too in the religious affairs of the church and parish of Malmesbury.

The present church at Sherborne far exceeds anything that Aldhelm could have built in size and grandeur. His cathedral church was probably a modest stone edifice of which nothing, except perhaps the foundations, now remains. But in subsequent generations the building was enlarged and by the end of the Saxon period it stood, a magnificent House of God, about the length of the church of today. To the present day sightseer the interesting and quaint little town is a joy to visit. But in the twelfth century William of Malmesbury thought little of it and considered it quite unworthy of having been the seat of a bishopric. He writes, "Sherborne is a village, possessing no attraction in number of inhabitants nor in charm of situation; it is a wonder, even a shame, that an episcopal see should have been held there during so many centuries." If Sherborne had no "charm of situation" itself, it was certainly the centre of one of the most beautiful dioceses in all England. It comprised the counties of Dorset, Somerset, Devon and, as the Saxons pressed westwards, parts of Cornwall.

(i) Lichfield Cathedral.   *Rackhams of Lichfield (the photographers)*

(ii)   Interior of Lichfield Cathedral.   *Rackhams of Lichfield (the photographers)*

uitur· Uae autem uobis scribae &
farissei hippocritae quia claudistis reg
num caelorum ante hominis uos autem
non intratis hec introeuntes siñetis intrar
re· Uae uobis scribae &farissei hi
pochritae quia circuin ias mare &aridam
ut faciatis unum proselitum &cum fue
rit factus facitis eum filium gehennae
duplo quam uos uae uobis duces cea
quid dicitis qui cum que iurauerit intem
plum nihil est qui autem iurauerit in
aurum templi debitor est stulta &cea
quid enim maius est aurum aurtemplu
quod sanctificat aurum &qui cumque iu
rauerit inaltare nihil est qui autem iu
rauerit indono quod est super illud
debitor est cea quid enim maiusest do
num an altare quod sanctificat donum
qui ergo iurat inaltare iurat ineo &in
omnibus quae super illud sunt &qui

(iii)   Page from St Chad's Gospels.
By permission of the Dean and Chapter of Lichfield Cathedral

(iv) Much Wenlock Priory.

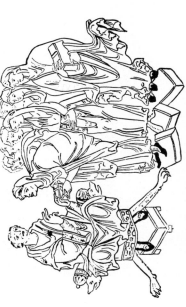

(vi) St Aldhelm presenting his treatise on virginity to the nuns of Barking.

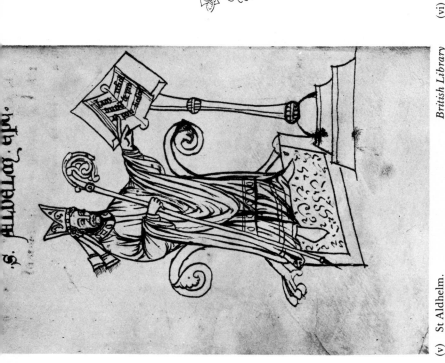

(v) St Aldhelm.

British Library

(vii)   Dorchester on Thames Abbey church.

(viii)   Sherborne Abbey.

(ix) Wimborne Minster.

S. F. James, F.I.I.P., R. A. Pink, A.I.I.P., Wimborne Minster

(x) Wimborne Minster interior.

S. F. James, F.I.I.P., R. A. Pink, A.I.I.P., Wimborne Minster

CHAPTER FOUR

St Cuthberga and Wimborne Minster

ADISTINCTIVE feature of the Anglo-Saxon Church of the seventh and eighth centuries was the double minster, which housed and trained both monks and nuns under the direction of an abbess, usually of royal birth. Apart from the double minsters there were, of course, all over England, numerous religious houses, some exclusively for women and others for men. But the popularity of the double monastery is evidenced by the large number of such foundations that grew up in England and on the Continent, many of them famed for their devotion, learning and missionary enterprise. In England such minsters existed at Barking, Coldingham, Ely, Much Wenlock, Repton, Whitby and Wimborne.

The founding of Wimborne Minster is recorded in the *Anglo-Saxon Chronicle* for the year 718. "In this year Ingild, Ine's brother died. Their sisters were Cwenburh and Cuthburh. And Cuthburh founded the monastery at Wimborne. She had been married to Aldfrith, king of the Northumbrians, and they separated during their lifetime." According to tradition the monastery was founded in about 713 or possibly earlier, the annal of the *Anglo-Saxon Chronicle,* 718, referring of course to Ingild's death.

How long Cuthberga had been married to Aldfrid (Aldfrith) when she left him for the cloister we do not know. Aldfrid became king of Northumbria in 685 so it is possible that the marriage had lasted for some years. As we have seen, Cuthberga entered the double monastery at Barking in Essex, governed then by the learned and energetic abbess, Hildilid. Aldhelm, her friend and kinsman, may have had some influence on the choice of Barking Minster for her training in the religious life. Barking had gained a high reputation for its devotion and learning in the time of Hildilid's predecessor, Ethelburga, its first abbess. She was the sister of Earconwald, bishop of London, a man of outstanding virtue for whom Aldhelm must have had respect and admiration. We find his name alongside that of Aldhelm on a contemporary charter. Earconwald had founded a monastery at Chertsey for monks and another for his sister, Ethelburga, at Barking. We know that this was a double monastery, for Bede writes of an outbreak of plague which attacked the men's part of the monastery.

Under the wise guidance of abbess Hildilid at Barking, Cuthberga would have studied the Scriptures and other subjects which comprised the curriculum of a double minster, special attention being given to the study and interpretation of the monastic Rule. It is likely that Cuthberga would have gained some knowledge of monastic life from Etheldreda, abbess of Ely, to whom she was related by marriage. Cuthberga's husband, Aldfrid, was the brother or half-brother of Etheldreda's husband, Egfrid; both men were kings of Northumbria, Aldfrid succeeding Egfrid.

After Cuthberga's training at Barking, which might have lasted for only one year, as Etheldreda's did at Coldingham, she returned to her native Wessex. The capital city, Winchester, was on a direct route, both by river or by the ancient Roman road, from Barking. Cuthberga's brother, Ine, still ruled the kingdom and provided land for the founding of a double minster such as that at Barking. It was to stand on the banks of the river Wym, a tributary of the Stour, and was about forty miles south west of Winchester. Wimborne, as we now know it, is situated in a sheltered valley and is thought to have been occupied by Roman troops attached to the garrison at Badbury Rings nearby. Numerous Roman remains have been discovered in the area, including pieces of mosaic under the floor of the minster.

It is through a surviving biography of one of Wimborne's most distinguished nuns, Leoba, that we learn something of the day-to-day affairs of the monastery. Unfortunately the author, Rudolph, tells us nothing of its first abbess, Cuthberga, nor of her sister Cwenburh, who most likely succeeded her as abbess. He does write in some detail, however, of a later abbess, Tette, also a sister of King Ine.

Tette was a strict, though not unkind, abbess who was resolved to protect her nuns from the slightest contact with men. Complete segregation was preserved between the monks and the nuns. The writer, in fact, refers to two communities, housed in separate quarters, both existing within the confines of the same high, stout walls. The nuns were never allowed in the monks' quarters or the monks in the nuns', except for the priests who celebrated Mass. As soon as Mass was over they were required to leave at once. Even bishops were not admitted into the nuns' quarters. The abbess herself, if she needed to speak with any of the monks, did so only through a window.

In dealing with the problems of human relationships within her community of nuns Tette showed wisdom, commonsense and generosity of spirit. This is illustrated in the way she dealt with some of the rebellious young nuns who were outraged by the harsh treatment they received from the prioress who was set over them and responsible for their training. Often they pleaded with her to rule them less strictly, but their pleas went unheeded and the prioress continued to impose her unyielding discipline upon the unhappy sisters.

It so happened that the prioress fell ill and died, and glad to be rid of such a tyrant, the young nuns gave vent to their feelings and trampled irreverently upon her grave, causing the soil to subside. At once the Abbess Tette checked their ill behaviour and rebuked them for their lack of charity, advising them to put aside all resentment against the prioress and to show a spirit of forgiveness.

But Tette herself was bound to admit that the prioress had been excessively harsh towards the young nuns and their hatred of her had not been altogether undeserved. Tette felt uneasy for the soul of the dead prioress. Prayers must be said for God's mercy and for the repose of her soul. Tette then summoned the nuns to join her in a three day fast and in prayers and the singing of litanies for the dead. And so it was done, the nuns praying and singing while Tette prostrated herself before the altar and wept and implored God's mercy for the soul of the prioress. Then all felt comforted and assured of her soul's absolution; and some declared that, as prayers were being said, the soil on her grave rose to its accustomed level.

Other wonderful tales were told of the Abbess Tette and the wisdom she showed in governing the monks and nuns of Wimborne Minster. We have mention of her, too, by a priest who had gone out from England to join the mission of Boniface to the Germans of Hesse and Saxony. His letter is addressed to the abbot and monks of Glastonbury but it is evident that he was well known at Wimborne and had perhaps been attached to that monastery at some time.

" . . . You know, brothers, that no earthly distance of land divides us whom the love of Christ unites. Therefore I am filled with brotherly love and reverence and with prayers for you to God. I wish you also to know, beloved brothers, that when our Archbishop Boniface heard of our arrival, he deigned to come himself a long way to meet us and receive us with great kindness . . . Living here is very perilous and full of hardship in almost every way, in hunger and thirst, in cold and the attacks of the pagans.

Therefore I ask earnestly: pray for us . . .
Farewell in the Lord. Greet the brothers round about, first abbot Ingild and our community, and send word to my mother Tette and her community of our safe journey . . . "*

The *Anglo-Saxon Chronicle* records that in 871 Ethelred, the king of Wessex, died and was buried at Wimborne. He and his younger brother Alfred had confronted the powerful Danish army at Ashdown in Berkshire and defeated the enemy. But in subsequent battles they suffered heavy losses, Ethelred, it is thought, dying from his wounds. A beautiful fifteenth century brass figure of the king in royal attire can be seen in the fine Minster Church of St Cuthberga in Wimborne. The brass is set into a slab of Purbeck marble and under it is an inscription telling of the king's death at the hands of the pagan Danes.

Wimborne Minster in the eighth century was important, not only for the training it gave to numerous men and women who were to serve the church in Wessex and other parts of England, but for the contribution it made towards the evangelization of the pagan tribes of the Continent under the leadership of St Boniface. In the next three chapters we shall examine the missionary endeavours of a few West Saxons, whose zeal for preaching the Gospel to the heathen inspired great numbers of their compatriots to leave their homeland, some never to return, to spread the Faith among the Germanic tribes of Central Europe. It was a missionary movement which owed its inspiration to the West Saxon Church and in particular to its first great missionary, St Boniface.

English Historical Documents. No. 182

CHAPTER FIVE

The West Saxon Mission to the Continent St Boniface, Apostle of Germany

L ESS than a hundred years after the Anglo-Saxons in Britain had been converted to Christianity they themselves were showing an eagerness to return to their continental homelands of Frisia and Germany to transmit their new-found faith to the tribes who were of the same stock as themselves. Their settlement in Britain had occurred not so far in the past as to cause a loss of identity with the pagan peoples of northern and central Europe. A sense of unity between the two peoples still existed.

The Anglo-Saxon mission to the Continent originated in the English kingdom of Northumbria towards the end of the seventh century. Wilfrid, bishop of York, was the first Englishman, as far as we know, who preached the Gospel to the pagan people of Frisia. He arrived there in the autumn of 678, his mission lasting for about six months. The real purpose of his journey to the Continent was to visit Rome; but his arrival in Frisia in the autumn made it unsafe for him to complete his journey across Europe during the treacherous conditions of winter. This was to turn out to the advantage of the Frisian people whose king, Aldgils, supported his missionary efforts. Many were baptised and accepted Wilfrid's message though the mission was too brief to bear any lasting fruit. In the spring he completed his journey to Rome. Wilfrid, however, had laid the foundation for the work of future missionaries. He was to be followed by one of his Northumbrian pupils, Willibrord, who, with eleven companions, worked for many years in Frisia under the authority of the pope and the patronage of the Frankish ruler, Pippin II.*

The work which had begun in Northumbria was taken up by men of Wessex, its most celebrated missionary being St Boniface of Crediton. Although he spent some years in Frisia working alongside Willibrord, his major achievement was among the Germanic people

---

*A fuller account of Willibrord's mission can be found in the Appendix

of Thuringia, Hesse and Bavaria and in the reform of the Frankish Church. In all these places he established well-organised churches based on the pattern of Rome. Like Willibrord, he had the authority and support of the papal see for all his missionary endeavours.

The history of Boniface's mission belongs more to the Continent than to England, yet we should remember that it was the English Church, and in particular that of Wessex, which gave him his early religious training. Throughout his years of missionary enterprise he continued to draw his inspiration from the Church which had nourished him. His surviving letters bear witness to this.

It is from his letters that much of our knowledge of Boniface is derived but we have a contemporary biography too, written by the priest, Willibald, (not to be confused with Willibald, bishop of Salzburg). The *Life of Boniface* was written in answer to a request, addressed by many of Boniface's friends, to Bishop Lull, his successor in the see of Mainz. One such request came from Milret, bishop of Worcester, who had been to Germany to visit Boniface not long before Boniface's martyrdom. His letter to Lull reads thus:

"To the kindly and beloved master in Christ, Bishop Lull, Milret, a servant of those who serve God.

After I had been obliged to leave your company and the presence of the holy father Boniface and returned, by the aid of your prayers, to my native land through divers accidents and many adventures, hardly a year had passed when the sad news was brought to us that our blessed father had passed from the prison of the flesh to the world above . . . Though we lament with bitter tears the comfort we have lost in this life, yet he who is now consecrated a martyr to Christ by the shedding of his blood, the glory and crown of all those whom this country has sent forth, soothes and relieves our saddened hearts by his blessed life, by the fulfilment of his noble work and his glorious end . . . He, his pilgrimage accomplished with mighty effort, attained to a glorious death as martyr of Christ . . . So much I write of our loving father. I beg you earnestly to send me an account of his venerable life and his glorious end.. . . "*

In response to the request, Bishop Lull and Bishop Megigoz of Wurzburg in central Germany appointed the priest Willibald to

The Anglo-Saxon Missionaries in Germany, The Correspondence of St Boniface. C. H. Talbot, from which all future quotations in this chapter are taken.

write the *Life of Boniface*. Willibald carried out his task within about fourteen years of the saint's death. He aimed at providing his readers, mostly monks and nuns, with an edifying account of Boniface's life which would serve them as an example.

Boniface, according to a fourteenth century tradition, was a native of Crediton in Devonshire. He was born in about 675 of noble parents who named their child Wynfrith. The Latin name Boniface, meaning well doer, was only given to him years later by Pope Gregory II, to mark the beginning of his mission to central Europe. To save confusion, however, we shall continue to use the name Boniface throughout the chapter.

Boniface was a boy of sharp intelligence. Itinerant preachers who were given lodging at his father's house were listened to with enthusiasm by him. They had come from one or other of the West Saxon monasteries, from Exeter perhaps, from Nursling, Glastonbury, or from Aldhelm's monastery at Malmesbury. Perhaps Aldhelm himself saw in the young Boniface a scholar of great promise. In his youth Boniface was an admirer of Aldhelm's elaborate literary style and attempted to imitate it. Some of his early letters show its influence but later, when he was grappling with the numerous problems of newly founded churches in Germany, he wrote in a straightforward style, far removed from that of Aldhelm.

From an early age Boniface showed an interest in the monastic life and wished to enter, as a pupil and oblate, one of the religious houses of Wessex. At first his father opposed the boy's notion, hoping that his son would follow a secular career and take over the running of the family estate. But Boniface showed little inclination for such a career and eventually won his father's agreement to place him in a monastery. He was sent to Exeter, not far from his home, and began his education under the abbot, Wulfhard, developing a keen interest in his literary and religious studies. Books became to him, as to Aldhelm, a source of endless pleasure, absorbing his mind in hours of study. Like Aldhelm too he found enjoyment in the composition of Latin verse and riddles and in studying the rules of grammar. This love of books never left him and in many of his letters to his friends at home, while he toiled in the mission fields of Germany, he made requests for this or that book to be sent to him.

After some years of study at Exeter, Boniface's enthusiasm for learning led him to seek the tuition of other excellent teachers. He found these at Nursling in Hampshire. The monastery which he now entered was governed by a scholarly abbot named Winbert, under whose tuition Boniface became proficient in many branches of learning, in particular a knowledge of the Scriptures and their meaning. Soon the level of scholarship to which he had attained equalled that of his masters and he was promoted to a place among them. His renown as a biblical scholar and his skill as a teacher soon became known outside of Nursling. Monks, and even nuns, came to sit at his feet and to listen to his wonderful exposition of the Scriptures. Those nuns who were unable to leave their cloisters to attend his lectures, but had heard of the excellence of his teaching, began to apply their minds to the study of the Scriptures and to meditate upon their meaning.

At Nursling Boniface won the affection and respect of his fellow monks. Though he was greatly above them in ability and knowledge, he humbly shared with them in the menial tasks of the monastery. The Rule of St Benedict, observed at Nursling, commanded that the brethren "be occupied at stated hours in manual labour, and again at other hours in sacred reading."

At about the age of thirty, Boniface was ordained to the priesthood, no doubt by his friend Bishop Daniel who administered the see of Winchester. In 705 the large West Saxon diocese had been divided, in accordance with the policy of the then archbishop of Canterbury, Bertwald, and his predecessor, Theodore. Aldhelm, as we have seen, administered the see of Sherborne, west of Selwood.

The division of the West Saxon diocese had been the cause of some disagreement and opposition within the kingdom itself. We have a letter of this date from Waldhere, bishop of London, to Bertwald, complaining of the failure of the West Saxons to obey the archbishop's "decree about the ordination of bishops". Willibald in his *Life of Boniface* also refers to a crisis within the West Saxon Church. To settle the affair King Ine summoned a council of churchmen to debate the matter. Willibald tells us nothing of the debate itself, his interest in it being confined to the part played by his hero, Boniface, whom he wished to exalt in the eyes of his readers.

King Ine brought the discussions to a conclusion and asked the clergy to choose a representative to report their decisions to the archbishop. The esteem in which Boniface was held by his fellow clergy is evidenced by their unanimous choice of him to act as legate to archbishop Bertwald. The king endorsed their choice and Boniface, with several companions, was sent off to Canterbury to put the matter before the archbishop. When he returned with Bertwald's reply, the King called a second council of clergy to discuss this reply. Boniface was a prominent member of the council and was present at a number of subsequent councils of the West Saxon Church. It looked as if he was suitable for high office in the English Church, a bishop perhaps, or an archbishop.

Boniface's mind, however, was preoccupied with other thoughts. He had for some time been concerned about the pagan tribes of the Continent, the Germanic people from whom the English race had sprung. Willibrord, he knew, was at work among the pagans of Frisia and other Englishmen had followed him. Wilfrid of York was dead now but the eagerness of his missionary spirit was alive still in the English Church. Boniface had heard how the pagans of Sussex owed their conversion to him, and overseas he was the first missionary to preach in Frisia. Wilfrid's travels through Europe had opened his eyes to the state of the Frankish Church and the widespread paganism among the Germanic tribes to the east. There was no lack of information on the state of Europe at the time. Boniface listened, with concern, to all that he heard from pilgrims and travellers, missionaries and traders. His spirit was stirred with enthusiasm to join the throngs of wayfarers for Christ who had left all to preach the Gospel to the heathen. To those in the heart of Europe, the people of Bavaria, Hesse, Saxony and Thuringia he felt especially drawn.

He revealed his longing to the wise and kindly abbot, Winbert, and asked his permission to leave the monastery for work in the mission fields of Germany. Winbert was reluctant to lose a man of Boniface's gifts and qualities of character and, at first, withheld his permission. But when he saw the earnestness of Boniface's desire to work in foreign lands he consented to free him from his monastic ties and helped to equip him for the journey. In 716, accompanied by a few companions, Boniface set out from Wessex for the port of London and obtained passage on a ship bound for Frisia. From here, after meeting up with Willibrord, he would be able to penetrate into the heart of Germany where he intended to work.

Boniface had unfortunately landed in Frisia at a time of political unrest; the ruler of independent, or Eastern, Frisia, King Radbod, had driven Willibrord from his see of Utrecht. Although Boniface managed to gain an audience with King Radbod he received little encouragement from him since Radbod vigorously opposed Christianity and had destroyed many of Willibrord's churches and restored pagan worship in his land.

It may help the reader at this point to be given a brief outline of the political situation against which we should see the missionary activities of Willibrord and Boniface. The dominant rulers in western Europe were the Franks whose kingdom extended far beyond that of present day France and included Belgium, parts of Holland, and Germany. Because of the weakness and corruption of the Merovingian kings (a dynasty named after its legendary founder, Merovech) real power lay in the hands of the Mayors of the Palace. These were originally stewards of the royal household but gradually assumed considerable political power. They ruled the two major political states, Neustria in the north west and Austrasia in the east. Austrasia emerged as the dominant state and, with the decline of the Merovingian dynasty, a new dynasty, the Arnulfings or Carolingians, arose from the noble Austrasian family of Arnulf. The grandson of Arnulf, Pippin II of Heristal, after defeating the Neustrians in the battle of Tertry in 687, became ruler of a united Frankland. He it was who supported the work of Willibrord in Frisia. Hostile neighbours however, Saxony to the east and Frisia in the north, disturbed the peace of Frankland. Although western Frisia had fallen into Frankish hands, to the east lay independent Frisia over which Radbod retained control. Raids across the border indicated his ambition to gain control also of western Frisia. By the time Pippin died in 714 the shadow of another invader, the Moor, fell ominously over Frankland from the direction of Spain.

Pippin was succeeded by his son, Charles Martel, a brilliant military leader and able statesman who governed the Franks until 741. In the famous battle of Poitiers in 732 he drove the Moors out of Frankish territory, back into Spain, thus saving western Europe from Muslim invasion. He was a friend of both Willibrord and Boniface and encouraged their missionary activities though he was less keen on the reform of his own Frankish Church and attached little importance to the ecclesiastical authority of Rome. Of his three sons, Carloman, Griffo and Pippin the Short, the latter emerged as king of the Franks (751-767) being anointed to the office by Boniface. With the ascent to the throne of Pippin the Short's son, Charles the Great, better known as Charlemagne, a new age of European history dawned.

To return now to our account of Boniface, he found himself, in 716, facing a hostile reception in Radbod's kingdom of Frisia, while Willibrord was living quietly in his monastery at Echternach. But not only was there hostility in Frisia; the whole of Frankland was in ferment. After the death of Pippin, rivalry for the succession tore the dynasty apart, Charles Martel being thrown into prison to prevent his accession to power. Boniface knew the absolute necessity for missionary preachers to gain the support of secular rulers in the territories where they wished to work. Until the Frankish kingdom had become more stable there was no future for his work. He therefore returned to England to the monastery at Nursling.

The brethren welcomed his return and when, soon after, the abbot, Winbert, died they appealed to Boniface to become their abbot. Boniface wished above all to fulfil his duty to the community at Nursling to which he owed so much. It was essential that the brethren should be ruled by an abbot who was agreeable to them and one whom they had chosen. Yet the call of the mission field could not be stifled. He had set his heart upon it. "Go ye into all the world and preach the Gospel," had been our Lord's command. The conflict was resolved when a suitable abbot, acceptable to the brethren, was found to rule the community.

In 718 Boniface set out once more for foreign lands. He carried with him letters of commendation to present to religious and secular rulers. One was from his friend Bishop Daniel.

"To godly and merciful kings, all dukes, reverend and beloved bishops, priests and holy abbots and to all the spiritual sons of Christ, Daniel, a servant of the servants of God.

Though the commandments of God should be observed by all the faithful with sincerity and devotion, Holy Scriptures lays special stress on the obligation of offering hospitality to travellers and shows how pleasing to God is the fulfilment of this duty . . .

So it will redound to your eternal welfare if you extend to the bearer of this letter, Wynfrith, [Boniface] a holy priest and servant of almighty God, a warm welcome such as God loves and enjoins. In receiving the servants of God you receive Him whom they serve, for he promised: 'He who receiveth you, receiveth me'."

Boniface landed at Boulogne. Stability had by now been restored to the Frankish kingdom. Charles Martel had escaped from prison and, by popular acclaim, become ruler of the Franks. Boniface did not at once, as we might have expected, seek to gain Charles' protection for the work he hoped to undertake. It was more important to him to gain the authority and support of the pope, as Willibrord had done. The English Church owed its origin to Rome and to the initiative of Pope Gregory the Great who had sent missionaries to preach to her people. Any future work that Boniface intended to do among the pagan tribes of Europe must be established on the same footing, and any churches established must follow the pattern of Rome. This attachment to the see of Rome was to continue throughout Boniface's ministry, as is evidenced by his numerous letters to a succession of popes and their replies to him.

From Boulogne, Boniface and his companions set off for Rome. The long trek across France, through the mountain passes of the Alps, into Lombardy and from thence south to Rome, would have taken some weeks to accomplish. In Rome they joined the crowds of pilgrims praying at the shrine of St Peter. They were guests, we may suppose, at one of Rome's many monasteries. A few days later Boniface was granted an audience with the pope, Gregory II, to whom he gave the letters of commendation from Bishop Daniel and others and discussed with him the mission he had in mind. The pope was impressed by the sincerity of Boniface and recalled him for talks on many days following to make a thorough investigation of the possibilities of such a mission. Finally Boniface was commissioned by Gregory to make a preliminary survey of those areas, inhabited by Germanic tribes, which he proposed to evangelize. He was then to send his report to the pope. This would give Gregory a clear idea of the extent of paganism and the problems involved in the proposed mission of evangelism. The pope gave Boniface a letter of authority for his work, dated 15th May 719. Until now Boniface had been known by his Saxon name Wynfrith. The name used in the letter is Boniface, which is evidence that it was given to him by the pope on this occasion to mark the beginning of his apostolic work of preaching the Gospel to the heathen. I quote only part of Gregory's long letter.

"Gregory, the servant of the servants of God, to Boniface, a holy priest.

Your holy purpose, as it has been explained to us, and your well-tried faith lead us to make use of your services in spreading the Gospel, which by the grace of God has been committed to our care. Knowing that from your childhood you have been a student of Sacred Scripture and that you now wish to use the talent entrusted to you by God in dedicating yourself to missionary work, we rejoice in your faith and desire to have you as our colleague in this enterprise. Wherefore, since you have humbly submitted to us your plans regarding the mission . . . we now place your humble and devout work upon a secure basis and decree that you go forth to preach the Word of God to those people who are still bound by the shackles of paganism."

On the return journey to Germany Boniface stayed for a time with the king of the Lombards, Liudbrand, who later allied himself to Charles Martel in his struggle against Moorish invaders. Only a few years before Boniface's visit to the king, the aged abbot of the monasteries at Monkwearmouth and Jarrow in Northumbria, on his way to Rome, had been recommended to Liudbrand by the Frankish king, Chilperic II. But the abbot, Ceolfrith, was taken ill in Burgundy and died before ever staying with Liudbrand or reaching Rome. Boniface must surely have known about Ceolfrith's journey by means of the many contacts that he and the people of Wessex had with Northumbria. The twin monasteries of Monkwearmouth and Jarrow were among the largest and most important in England and, at the time of Ceolfrith's abbacy, housed about six hundred monks.

From Lombardy Boniface journeyed into Bavaria and northwards into Thuringia to the east of the Rhine. Thuringia was part of the Frankish Empire and had once received some Christian teaching from Frankish priests. Celtic clergy had also worked in Thuringia in the seventh century but the weakness of the Celtic Church lay in its lack of central organisation and their work left no lasting impression. When Boniface came to preach in Thuringia at the beginning of the eighth century the Church was in a decadent state; heresy was widespread, the clergy indolent and immoral and the common folk returning once more to their pagan practices. On this preliminary visit Boniface met religious leaders, reproving those clergy who had forsaken their vows of celibacy and taken wives, or who were living in fornication. Secular leaders, too, were recalled "to the true way of knowledge and the light of understanding which, for the greater part, they had lost through the perversity of their teachers."

News of the death of Radbod, the pagan ruler of independent Frisia, in 719, caused Boniface to change his immediate plan to work in central Europe. He had not forgotten his attempt in 716 to join Archbishop Willibrord in Utrecht. Now at last the opportunity had arisen for him to join the Frisian mission and to learn some lessons in the art of evangelism from that wise and experienced missionary, Willibrord. Frisia came now under the complete control of Charles Martel but was ruled by his vassal, Aldgils II, son of Radbod. Unlike his father, Aldgils was a devout Christian who encouraged the advance of the Faith in Frisia. For three years Boniface worked alongside Willibrord and his missionary team, preaching, destroying pagan shrines and building churches.

During these three years, 719-722, Boniface corresponded with friends in England. To the abbess of a minster he wrote asking for a copy of *The Sufferings of the Martyrs*. She replied that she was unable to obtain a copy but would send one as soon as she was able. She continually thanked God for guarding him as he travelled through strange and distant lands and for inspiring the pope to agree to his heartfelt desire to preach to the heathen. The letter to her and other abbesses and nuns, shows how deeply Boniface valued their friendship and encouragement, their prayers and practical help. Their letters in turn express the great respect, admiration and affection they felt towards this devoted and courageous West Saxon missionary.

Willibrord, now about sixty-five years old, saw in Boniface outstanding qualities of character and powers of leadership. He could wish for no one more suitable than Boniface to succeed him as bishop of Utrecht with responsibility for the Church in Frisia. Boniface, however, refused to accept "so exalted and sublime an office". Was he not committed to preach the Faith to the pagans of Germany, in the lands to which he had originally been despatched by the Holy See? Of course Willibrord knew that Boniface was right; he must fulfill the papal command. So Willibrord gave him his blessing and sent him on his way.

Boniface left Frisia and travelled up the Rhine until he reached the province of Hesse. At Amoeneburg, a few miles east of Marburg, he established a base which was to become a centre of his missionary activity. In this area too, was Fulda where he was later to found a monastery. At Amoeneburg he won the support of two chieftains, the brothers Dettic and Devrulf, whom he turned from the worship of idols to the true Faith. As was customary many ordinary folk followed the lead of their ruler and abandoned idolatry, accepting Christianity. Encouraged by the response to his message Boniface built a small chapel there for public worship.

The advance of Christianity in Hesse, due to the preaching of Boniface and his team of helpers, was so rapid and successful that he judged this to be the right time to report to the pope on the progress of his work. He sent a messenger to Rome with a full account of what had so far been accomplished and of the thousands who had responded to their preaching. Boniface also asked for the pope's ruling on various moral and ecclesiastical problems. The pope replied by summoning Boniface to Rome.

The pope was clearly gratified at the success of Boniface's preliminary mission and had in mind the intention of consecrating him bishop. He wished first to be certain of the orthodoxy of Boniface's faith. When the two met, Gregory questioned him on the doctrines and creeds of the Church. On so important a matter

Boniface requested that he might be allowed to present to the pope a written statement of his beliefs. Though a competent Latin scholar, Boniface lacked fluency in the colloquial Latin spoken in Rome at the time. Gregory agreed to this and sent Boniface away to compose his statement. On its completion Gregory was completely satisfied as to the orthodoxy of Boniface's beliefs. The two men now went on to discuss various religious matters and the problems concerning the mission. Gregory was well aware of its importance and told Boniface of his wish to consecrate him bishop. As such he would have authority to ordain priests, to carry out other episcopal functions and to found a Church in accordance with the wishes of Rome. His episcopal status would, too, win him the respect and support of secular rulers in whose territory he was to work.

Boniface was consecrated bishop by Pope Gregory II on 30th November 722, or as some believe, in 723. The book of Canon Law was placed in his hands, the pope commanding him to uphold the faith of the Church in its doctrine and morals and to teach the same to those under his care. Among the surviving letters and documents relating to his mission is the oath of obedience taken by Boniface at the time of his consecration. Part of this oath reads:

"In the name of God and of our Saviour Jesus Christ . . .

I, Boniface, by the grace of God bishop, promise to you, blessed Peter, chief of the Apostles, and to your vicar, the blessed Pope Gregory, and to his successors, in the name of the indivisible Trinity, Father, Son and Holy Ghost, and on thy most sacred body, that I will uphold the faith and purity of holy Catholic teaching and will persevere in the unity of the same faith in which beyond doubt the whole salvation of a Christian lies . . .

Should it come to my notice that some bishops deviate from the teaching of the Fathers I will have no part or lot with them, but as far as in me lies I will correct them, or, if that is impossible, I will report the matter to the Holy See . . . "

An important collection of letters has survived from this early period of Boniface's work. Those from the pope are addressed to religious and secular leaders, clergy and laity in different parts of the Frankish Empire and were given to Boniface to deliver either to particular individuals or to be shown to clergy and their congregations in various districts. They are important for the light they throw on the mission as a whole and for an understanding of the complexity of the problems involved in it.

To the German Christians in general the pope writes:

" . . . We exhort you, then, for the love of our Lord Jesus Christ and the reverence you bear to his apostles, to support him [Boniface] by all means at your disposal and to receive him in the name of Jesus Christ . . . See to it that he has all he requires; give him companions to escort him on his journey, provide him with food and drink and anything else he may need, so that with the blessing of God the work of piety and salvation committed to him may proceed without hindrance."

A letter written by the pope, addressed to the clergy and people of Thuringia, tells them of Boniface's episcopal consecration and of those matters of ecclesiastical custom which he must uphold. He is to ordain only those men who are in good physical health, married according to the Church's ruling and orthodox in their faith. He is to see that church buildings are properly furnished and adorned. He is to divide the offerings of the faithful and any other church revenue equally between himself, his clergy, pilgrims and the poor and the upkeep of church fabrics. Baptisms must take place at Easter and Whitsun and ordinations in April, July, October and the beginning of Lent.

The pope wrote to Charles Martel, now supreme ruler of the Frankish Empire.

"To the glorious Lord, our son, Duke Charles.

Having learned, beloved son in Christ, that you are a man of deeply religious feeling, we make known to you that our brother Boniface, who now stands before you, a man of sterling faith and character, has been consecrated bishop by us, and after being instructed in the teachings of the Holy Apostolic See, over which by God's grace we preside, is being sent to preach the Faith to the peoples of Germany who dwell on the eastern bank of the Rhine, some of whom are still steeped in the errors of paganism . . .

For this reason we commend him without more ado to your kindness and goodwill, begging you to help him in all his needs and to grant him your constant protection against any who may stand in his way . . . "

Boniface left Rome, prepared now to continue in earnest his missionary efforts among the German people. He had the pope's unequivocal support for this work, he carried the letters of commendation and he had been raised to the rank of bishop. He went first to Charles Martel to gain his backing for the mission and his promise of protection. The pope's letter was given to Charles and he, in turn, stated, in a letter to his officials and subjects, his intention of granting protection to Boniface.

"Let it be known that the apostolic father, Bishop Boniface, has come into our presence and begged us to take him under our protection. Know then that it has been our pleasure to do this.
Furthermore we have seen fit to issue and seal with our own hand an order that wheresoever he goes, no matter where it shall be, he shall with our love and protection remain unmolested and undisturbed . . . "

Boniface now returned to his base at Amoeneburg in Hesse and prepared for a preaching tour of the province. Christianity had earlier been preached in Hesse and many had received baptism but Boniface still found there a deep attachment to heathen customs and beliefs. It was here in Hesse that he felled the sacred oak which had been venerated for centuries by the local people. It was an act, symbolic of the destruction of an age-old pagan faith and the inauguration of a new, for as the ancient tree crashed to the ground it revealed within its crumbling trunk signs of sturdy new growth. This sight delighted the hitherto angry crowd who now gave greater attention to the preacher's message. Boniface concluded the episode by ordering a chapel dedicated to St Peter to be built from the timber of the fallen oak.

The pope was kept informed about the progress of the mission in Hesse and sent a letter of encouragement to Boniface. The letter is dated 4th December 723.

"To his most reverend brother and fellow bishop, Boniface, Gregory, the Servant of the servants of God.
. . . Do not be frightened by threats or discouraged by fears. Keep your trust fixed on God and proclaim the word of truth. Provided your will is constant in good works, God will crown it by His help . . .
As for the bishop who was too lazy to preach the Word of God and now claims part of your diocese, we have written to our son, Duke Charles, asking him to restrain him, and we believe that he will put a stop to it . . . "

From Hesse Boniface moved on into Thuringia where heretical priests had been spreading erroneous doctrines. Asserting his authority as a bishop, Boniface banished the priests from the country and, with the help of his team of preachers, began to instruct the people in the orthodox teachings of the Church. His work flourished. "Little by little the numbers of believers increased, the preachers grew more numerous, church buildings were restored and the Word of God was published far and wide." A monastery was founded at Ohrdruf, near the present day Gotha, the first of a number founded in Germany by Boniface and his successors. These were to become important centres of devotion, learning and missionary enterprise.

Boniface wrote to Pope Gregory II for guidance on numerous problems that arose as the Faith advanced in Hesse and Thuringia. Gregory replied with his instructions, some more lenient, others more severe than we might have expected. If a man's wife, through illness, is unable to fulfil her duties as a wife, he may marry again if he finds continence impossible, though he must continue to support the sick wife. Children who have been consecrated to the cloister are forbidden to forsake their vows after puberty and to marry. Priests and bishops whose vicious lives are a reproach to the priesthood must be admonished and corrected and brought back to the purity of ecclesiastical discipline. "If they obey, they will save their souls, and you, on your side, will attain your reward."

It is evident from Willibald's biography and from Boniface's own correspondence that his life in the mission field was fraught with danger, hardship and anxiety. Willibald tells of his deep distress, extreme want and lack of bare necessities. To Nothelm, archbishop of Canterbury, Boniface writes, "I earnestly beg you to remember me in your holy prayers and so bring peace to my mind, tossed as it is by the anxieties of this mission in Germany." To the abbess of an English minster he writes asking for her prayers, "because for my sins I am wearied with my trials and vexed in body and mind." And, as the years advanced, he writes to a former pupil, "Be mindful of my devotion and take pity on an old man, worn out by troubles in this German land. Support me by your prayers."

As news of Boniface's mission reached Britain many new recruits came out to join him. They were men of various gifts; writers, scholars, teachers, and those trained in practical skills. Women, too, came from the English minsters and helped to establish religious houses in Germany. Boniface wrote to the abbess, Tette of Wimborne, asking her to send his kinswoman, Leoba, to help him in the mission field. As we shall see, Leoba was a woman of rare gifts and strong character who became abbess of the house at Bischofsheim. These new recruits, with their variety of talents, must have greatly enriched the lives of the pagan people among whom they worked, bringing them, not only the Christian religion, but education and learning too.

In 731 Pope Gregory II died and was succeeded by Gregory III. Boniface wrote asking him for the continued friendship and support of the papal see. The new pope replied, assuring him of that friendship and congratulating him on his success in the mission field. He told Boniface that it was the wish of the papal see to raise him to the rank of archbishop with authority to consecrate bishops. At these consecration ceremonies and at Mass he was to wear the pallium which was being sent to him from Rome. The burden of work upon himself would be lightened, said the pope, if he increased the number of bishops; but he must take care to consecrate only men of tried worth "so that the dignity of the episcopate may not fall into disrepute." It seems that at this stage, perhaps because of his continual journeying from place to place, Boniface was no more than a regionary archbishop and had no fixed episcopal seat. Not until 747 was he known as archbishop of Mainz.

Encouraged by Gregory's letter and the many gifts sent from Rome, Boniface made plans to extend his work into the province of Bavaria. But first he built churches and monasteries at Amoeneburg and Fritzlar. He consecrated more bishops to continue the work in Hesse and Thuringia and sent out groups of preachers to the villages and country districts.

Boniface's first visit to Bavaria bore no great fruit, the ruler being unwilling to support his work. He was able, however, to make a tour of the country and the centres of church life and to rid the land of heretical teachers, chief among them Eremwulf. It was clear to him that a complete reorganisation of the Bavarian Church was needed. It would be an immense task and for this he must have the advice and support of Rome. He decided on a third visit to the Holy See so that he might meet the new pope and discuss with him, among other matters, the needs of the Bavarian Church and his hope of evangelizing the Saxons.

In 738, when he was about sixty-two or three, Boniface made the journey to Rome and stayed there for about a year. He was received with great kindness by the pope and must have discussed in some detail his missionary plans for the future. We do not hear of Boniface carrying out a mission to the Saxons though Willibald, his biographer, may have failed to mention such a mission. In a letter to Christians in England Boniface asks them to pray for the conversion of the pagan Saxons for "we are of one and the same blood and bone." Christian Saxons from Britain were among the hordes of pilgrims in Rome at the time Boniface was there. When he was invited to preach in the city crowds came to hear him including Franks, Bavarians, Saxons and natives of Rome. All paid the closest attention to his teaching.

In 739 Boniface returned to Bavaria and, assisted by the new ruler, Duke Odilo, embarked upon the reform and reorganisation of the Bavarian Church. Four dioceses were created: Salzburg, Regensburg, Freising and Passau. The latter already had its bishop, Vivilo, but Boniface consecrated three more to serve in the other sees. In 741 a further bishopric was created at Eichstatt, an Englishman, Willibald, becoming its first bishop. In the autumn of 739 Pope Gregory III wrote to Boniface about his work in Bavaria giving him instructions on various questions of Church discipline.

" . . . You tell us that you have made a journey into Bavaria and found the people there living in a manner contrary to the ordinances of the Church and that because they have no bishops except Vivilo, whom we consecrated some time ago, you have, with the approval of Odilo, Duke of Bavaria, and the nobles of the province, consecrated three other bishops. You say also that you have divided the province into four districts, so that each bishop may have his own diocese. In carrying out our commands and in performing the task that was enjoined upon you, you have acted well.

Continue, reverend brother, to teach them the holy, Catholic and Apostolic traditions of the See of Rome, so that the ignorant may be enlightened and may follow the path that leads to eternal bliss . . . "

The pope continues with instructions that priests must be re-ordained if the validity of their orders is under suspicion. Bishop Vivilo must be instructed in the true faith if he has deviated from orthodoxy. Boniface is to consecrate bishops where there is need and continue to preach the Faith among the heathen so long as his strength permits and, he says, "Do not shrink, beloved brother, from difficult and protracted journeys in the service of the Christian Faith".

Boniface's letters to his English friends are of particular interest. He writes to Bishop Daniel about his difficulties and vexations of mind, asking for his judgements and advice. He is obliged to attend the Frankish court, he says, and if he does not do so his missionary work will suffer. In doing so, however, he is compelled to have contact with false priests who lead people astray by their scandalous lives and heretical teaching. At his consecration he had taken an oath, promising to avoid their company if he could not bring them back to the right path. What is Daniel's judgement on the matter? And could he please send him the copy of the *Book of the Prophets* which had belonged to Winbert, abbot of Nursling: "It cannot be procured in this country, and with my failing sight it is impossible for me to read small, abbreviated script."

He writes to Archbishop Egbert of York asking for some of the writings of Bede; to Hwaetberht, abbot of Monkwearmouth and Jarrow for a cloak for use on his journeys and he asks for the abbot's prayers to help him and his fellow workers "in our labours among the rude and savage people of Germany, where we are sowing the seed of the Gospel." He writes to Nothelm, archbishop of Canterbury, and asks for a copy of Augustine's questions to Gregory I. He wants to know, too, whether the document is authentic. From the king of Kent, Ethelbert, he receives a letter requesting a pair of falcons "quick and spirited enough to catch crows . . . since there are few hawks of this kind over here in Kent." With this letter came the gift for Boniface of two cloaks and a silver drinking cup lined with gold.

In 741 Charles Martel died. He had encouraged Boniface's missionary activity in Frisia and Germany but had been less interested in the reform of the Church in his own Frankish kingdom. For this work Boniface received the patronage of Charles' two sons, Carloman and Pippin. Both had been educated in the monastic school at St Denis near Paris and were eager to give their support to a reform movement in their respective kingdoms, Austrasia ruled by Carloman and Neustria by Pippin.

In a letter to Pope Zacharias (741-752), who had succeeded Gregory III, Boniface speaks of a synod which Carloman wishes to convene in Austrasia to discuss the reform of the Church. For over sixty years, he says, ecclesiastical discipline has been disregarded, no councils have been held, canon law has been flouted, no archbishops have been appointed and bishoprics in the cities have been placed in the hands of priests of immoral life. There are deacons who, though indulging in debauchery, read the Gospel in church and continue in their careers of vice even when priested. Some bishops too are "shiftless drunkards, addicted to the chase."

The pope, in reply, denounces the conduct of the Frankish clergy and gives Boniface authority to suspend them from priestly duties and from the celebration of Mass. "How do they think they can perform priestly duties when they are obviously steeped in such crimes as are unthinkable even in laymen? Are they not afraid to handle the sacred mysteries? How can they have the effrontery to offer prayers for the sins of the people?"

The first of the Synods was held in 742 in the presence of Carloman and presided over by Boniface. It was the first step towards the reform of the Frankish Church and resulted in a number of important decisions. Synods were to be held every year, heretical clergy were to be deprived of their office, unlawful marriages of clergy were to be annulled and priests were to make annual reports to their bishops.

In 743 a second synod was held in Austrasia. The following year Pippin presided over a synod in his own province of Neustria and in 745 a joint synod was held for both Austrasian and Neustrian churchmen. The pattern had been set now for the convening of annual synods.

Carloman had always been a deeply religious man and in 747 he renounced political power and went to Rome to receive the monastic tonsure from Pope Zacharias, eventually becoming a monk at Monte Cassino. The government of the entire kingdom now fell to his younger brother, Pippin, known as Pippin the Short. He was king in everything but name, his official title still being Mayor of the Palace. The title of king belonged to Childeric III. At once an envoy was sent to Rome to enquire of the pope whether it was not right that the man who ruled the kingdom should not also hold the title of king. The pope replied that this was so and advised that Pippin should be crowned. Accordingly in 751 Childeric was deposed and Pippin III was crowned king of the Franks by Archbishop Boniface. The fact that Pippin did not assume the title of king without reference to Rome demonstrates his acknowledgement of the authority of the pope over the Frankish Church and his wish to maintain cordial relations with the papal see. It was the beginning of an alliance between the Frankish Empire and the papacy which was to characterise the reign and achievements of Pippin's son Charlemagne.

A few years before Carloman had abdicated and retired to a monastery he had made a generous grant of land to Boniface on the banks of the river Fulda, in eastern Hesse. It was to be the site of Boniface's largest and most important monastery and, for himself, a place of rest and refreshment amidst all the anxieties of his episcopal duties. The first abbot was Sturm, one of Boniface's disciples and fellow workers, under whom the monastery was to rise to great fame as a centre of religion, culture and learning, housing as many as four hundred monks. Of Fulda Boniface wrote to Pope Zacharias in 751.

"There is a wooded place in the midst of a vast wilderness situated among the peoples to whom I am preaching. There I have placed a group of monks living under the rule of St Benedict who are building a monastery. They are men of ascetic habits, who abstain from meat and wine and spirits, keeping no servants, but are content with the labour of their own hands . . . Here I propose with your kind permission to rest my aged and worn body for a little time, and after my death to be buried there . . . "

Boniface was by now nearing the age of eighty. Physical infirmity often prevented him from attending synods. It was time, he thought, to appoint a successor. With the king's permission he chose Lull, one of his early recruits from England who had been educated at Malmesbury. In a letter to the king's chaplain, Fulrad, abbot of St Denis, Boniface writes of the need for a successor to be appointed so that his disciples may not lack pastoral care.

"It seems to me, considering my ill-health, that this mortal life of mine and the daily course of my activities must soon come to an end. Therefore I pray His Royal Highness, in the name of Christ, the Son of God, to indicate while I am still alive what future provision he is willing to make for my disciples. They are nearly all foreigners. Some are priests spending their lives in lonely places in the service of the Church and people. Some are monks in cloisters or children learning to read. Others are men of mature age who have been my companions and helpers for many years. My chief anxiety about all of them is that after my death they may have to disperse and be scattered abroad like sheep without a shepherd, unless they have the support and patronage of Your Highness . . . For this reason I earnestly beg Your Gracious Highness to have my son, the auxiliary bishop Lull, appointed in place, as preacher and teacher to the priests and people . . . "

The king complied with Boniface's request and Lull was consecrated archbishop of Mainz. One would have thought that Boniface, now free from episcopal duties, would have retired to the monastery at Fulda as he had planned. But the missionary spirit still burned within him and it seems he could not rest until he had paid one last visit to the land of Frisia where he had first begun his missionary activity. This, he felt, would be his last journey on earth. To Lull he wrote:

> "The day of my departure from this life draws near and the time of my death is approaching. In a short time I shall lay aside the burden of my body and receive the prize of eternal bliss. But do thou, dear son, bring to completion the building of the churches which I began in Thuringia. Earnestly recall the people from the paths of error, finish the construction of the basilica at Fulda, which is now in process of building, and bring hither this body of mine now wasted by the toil of years."

In 753, with a few companions, he sailed from Mainz down the Rhine into the flat marshy country of Frisia and across the Zuyder Zee. Many of the people he found still worshipping their pagan gods and with the help of Eoban, bishop of Utrecht, he conducted a mission among them. According to *The Life of Sturm* the mission lasted for two summers and many thousands were converted.

But enemies of Christianity, intent upon doing harm to Boniface and his team of helpers, lurked behind the scenes, awaiting their opportunity to rob and murder the Christians. A band of these pagan ruffians, hearing that Boniface was going to confirm a number of Christians at Dokkum, near Leeuwarden, on a certain day, made plans to attack him and his companions. On 5th June 754, as dawn broke, they burst in upon the camp of the Christian preachers furiously brandishing their weapons. Boniface had time only for a few words of encouragement to his companions and to order them to refrain from fighting. Then the frenzied band fell upon them, killing Boniface and about fifty of his followers. They ransacked their tents and carried off chests of books and holy relics thinking they contained gold and silver. From the ships they took the supplies of food and wine which the missionaries had brought with them and began to feast themselves. Then, drunk with the wine, they began to quarrel over the booty. The weapons which had been used against the Christian martyrs were now turned against each other. Those who survived, angry at finding no gold or silver, flung the books into the marshes and returned home. Later a number of these precious manuscripts were recovered and returned to the library at Fulda.

The bodies of the martyrs were taken to the Frisian city of Utrecht, that of Boniface first to his episcopal seat at Mainz and then to Fulda for burial, as he had requested. The monastery which he had founded in Fulda flourished, and, in the ninth and tenth centuries became one of Germany's most renowned centres of religion, art and learning. The learned Rabon Maur, author of the hymn "Veni Creator Spiritus", was abbot from 822-842. Fulda still remains an important ecclesiastical centre and an annual meeting place of bishops. In the crypt of the Cathedral, beneath the high altar is the tomb of St Boniface, patron saint of Germany. Though a large number of churches in Germany bear the name of Boniface in their dedications compared to the few in England we are right to number this great missionary among England's saints since he was an Englishman and a native of Wessex. He is remembered on 5th June in our Anglican Calendar.

CHAPTER SIX

The West Saxon Mission to the Continent Leoba, Abbess of Bishchofsheim

AMONG the noble and royal families of Anglo-Saxon England women occupied a place of prestige and importance. Queens had a decided influence upon their husbands and by their counsel could change the direction of policy. During interim periods they even governed the kingdoms themselves. Abbesses administered large communities of men and women in the double minsters and became the counsellors and friends of kings and queens, princes and noblemen, clergy and people. In the surge of enthusiasm for the religious life which followed the advent of the Christian missionaries' many English women devoted themselves to the cloister and achieved renown for their learning and piety.

Boniface was among those early English Churchmen who welcomed and valued the contribution which women could make to the life of the Church. His correspondence bears witness to the friendship he extended to many women of the cloister, nuns and abbesses. He believed that the English mission to the Continent would be greatly enhanced by the presence of some of these women among the new converts in Germany. He therefore appealed for recruits from the English minsters and in particular from the minster in his own native Wessex which he knew so well, Wimborne. And among those nuns of Wimborne whom he had in mind was Leoba to whom he was related on her mother's side and with whose father he had enjoyed a long friendship. Her reputation for holiness and learning had spread far and wide and "her praise was on everyone's lips." Boniface wrote to the abbess of Wimborne, Tette, to ask if Leoba might be sent out to join his mission.

Tette was hesitant. Leoba's good qualities of character and her intellectual gifts marked her out as a suitable successor in the abbacy of Wimborne. She was already a mistress of the novices, responsible for their instruction and training and a valuable influence on their developing personalities. It was understandable that Tette was reluctant to free Leoba. But the urgency of Boniface's appeal and the undoubted importance of his mission induced her to lay aside all other considerations and to send Leoba to Germany. Several other nuns were chosen to accompany her and to work alongside her in whatever place she was appointed to by Boniface. He chose to send her to Bischofsheim in the present day Baden where she would govern a community of nuns. Leoba's work at Bishchofsheim and its daughter houses, and her remarkable influence outside the cloister, led to many requests, after her death, for an account of her life. The result was *A Life of Leoba* written by a scholarly monk of Fulda, Rudolph, who was in charge of the monastic library. Leoba was a well known visitor to Fulda and had been commended to the senior monks there by Boniface.

Rudolph wrote his *Life of Leoba* in 836, over fifty years after her death. He tells us that the chief source of his information was the reminiscences of four of her pupils, Agatha, Thecla, Nana and Eoloba, which had been written down by several monks at Fulda, in particular by the priest, Mago. Rudolph's task of collating the facts of Leoba's life from scattered pieces of information, written down on odd pieces of parchment, was not an easy one. Mago's notes were especially difficult to decipher as they were written in a kind of shorthand of his own invention.

Rudolph relates first that Leoba was the only child of her parents, born to them in their old age, and therefore greatly cherished. Being devout Christians they brought up their child in a religious atmosphere and taught her the Scriptures from an early age. When she was old enough to leave her parents they placed her under the care of Abbess Tette at Wimborne in their own West Saxon country. "The girl therefore grew up and was taught with such care by the abbess and all the nuns that she had no interests other than the monastery and the pursuit of sacred knowledge. She took no pleasure in aimless jests and wasted no time on girlish romances, but, fired by the love of Christ, fixed her mind always on reading or hearing the Word of God."*

At some time in her early life she studied under the learned abbess, Eadburg, of Minster in Thanet, Kent. We gather this from a letter written by Leoba to Boniface. Rudolph makes no mention of this part of her education, either because he did not know of it or because he chose to omit it. The letter, written not earlier than 732, suggests a measure of maturity in both the content of the letter and in the writer's style. Leoba had already mastered Latin prose and was practising the art of writing verse, which had been taught to her

*The Anglo-Saxon Missionaries in Germany. C. H. Talbot

by Abbess Eadburg. Her father, Dynna, she says, has been dead for eight years and her mother is suffering from the infirmities of old age. She speaks of the kinship between her mother and Boniface and the longstanding friendship between him and her father. She asks for Boniface's prayers and says she would like to think of him as a brother "for in none of the men of my race have I placed so much faith and hope as in you."

If we piece together the information gleaned by this letter with what Rudolph says about her childhood, we are left with the impression that Leoba probably received her earliest education under Tette at Wimborne. Then she left the minster there for a period of study in Kent, and returned to Wimborne before being despatched to Germany. Rudolph says that Tette was the first person to introduce Leoba to the religious life and that as a girl she was taught by her and her nuns. It was a common practice for monks, and perhaps to a lesser extent, nuns, to study in more than one monastery, especially for those of intellectual ability. It would be quite in order for Leoba to be sent to Minster in Thanet for a period of study under the scholarly abbess, Eadburg. We are told that Leoba studied the Scriptures and their meaning and became acquainted with the writings of the Church Fathers and every aspect of ecclesiastical law. It is clear too, that she became a competent Latin scholar.

At Wimborne Leoba was put in charge of the young sisters, with responsibility for their training as novices. Rudolph relates how Leoba sent one of these young novices to enquire of a senior nun, who possessed the gift of prophecy, the meaning of an unusual dream. The young nun was told to relate the dream as if it had been her own. The aged sister listened to the account of the dream but at once perceived that it was Leoba, and not the young novice, who had had the dream. The purple thread which she had seen issuing from her mouth in the dream signified the wise sayings she would utter: these, like her good example, would bring benefit to many. "By these signs," said the aged nun, "God shows that your mistress will profit many by her words and example, and the effect of them will be felt in other lands afar off whither she will go."

The words of this wise old prophetess were to be fulfilled when Leoba, with Tette's permission, responded to Boniface's appeal for recruits to work in the mission fields of Germany. Boniface put Leoba in charge of a large community of nuns at Bischofsheim, sixty miles or so south of his own monastery at Fulda. During her years as abbess the convent gained a high reputation for devotion and learning and from its doors went out nuns, whom she had trained, to become abbesses of other German convents. A number of daughter houses of her own convent were also founded. Leoba was given overall charge of them and was responsible for their administration.

Rudolph, like other writers of Saints' Lives, draws special attention to the virtues of his subject. Leoba, he says, endeavoured to emulate those virtues which she most admired in her companions: the cheerfulness of one, the patience of another, the devotion to prayer of others. Above all she practised charity towards everyone. She was diligent and always occupied either in prayer, study or the performance of some manual task about the monastery.

Sir Frank Stenton has said of Leoba, "She was a women of most unusual personal charm, and the affection which Boniface felt for her introduces an element of ordinary human feeling into the record of his austere life." A letter written by Boniface to Leoba when both were in Germany illustrates this affection and shows the trust he placed in her judgement.

> "To the reverend handmaid in Christ, Leoba, held ever in sincere affection, Boniface, a servant of the servants of God, sends his heartfelt greetings in Christ.
>
> Be it known to you, dear sister, that our brother and fellow priest, Torhthat, has reported to us that, in response to his request, you are willing to permit a certain maiden to receive instruction for a time, if we give our consent.
>
> Be assured, therefore, that whatever you may see fit to do in this matter, for the increase of her merits, shall have our consent and approval. Farewell in Christ."

Leoba was single-minded in the service she rendered to the people of central Germany. From the outset of her work she vowed that she would not yearn after a return to her native land. Like Boniface himself she never saw England again. Her life was devoted to the ruling of her convent and the training of the sisters. But her influence reached beyond the cloister to many people outside. Guests were entertained, the house being open to all without discrimination between rich and poor, high and lowly. She delighted to provide banquets for others even though she herself was fasting, for she never wished to impose on others the strict rules she observed herself. Perhaps the greater freedom of the rule she followed at Bischofsheim was a reaction against the strict regime of Wimborne. Yet Rudolph leaves us in no doubt that Tette was a woman of wise and balanced judgement whose strict rule at Wimborne was tempered with kindness; and Leoba certainly had great respect and affection for her.

At Bischofsheim Leoba maintained her enthusiasm for learning, especially for study of the Scriptures and memorising them whenever possible. So thorough was her knowledge of the Scriptures that she could detect the slightest mistake a nun might make while reading to her at rest time. The nuns discovered that even while she slept her mind was on what they read and she would correct their smallest error. Study required the complete attention of the mind, she claimed, and to achieve this, adequate sleep was necessary. The sisters were never allowed to stay up too late at their prayers and devotions, for, she said, "lack of sleep dulls the mind, especially for study." In hot weather both she and her sisters took a period of rest after the midday meal.

The way in which Leoba dealt with a distressing situation involving her nuns was regarded by many as nothing short of miraculous. A crippled girl belonging to the district, who sat and begged at the convent gate and was given food and clothes by the sisters, was the cause of a local scandal. The girl, yielding to the advances of men, found that she had conceived a child. Ashamed of her condition she feigned sickness, stayed at home, and bore the child in secret. Then she threw the infant into the river where local people were accustomed to draw water. A village woman, seeing the dead child floating in the water, raised the alarm, accusing the nuns of Leoba's convent of the shameful deed. "These are fine nuns!" said the indignant woman, "who beneath their veils give birth to children and pollute the water with the corpses of their unlawful offspring." News spread round the village of this wicked crime and fingers of accusation were pointed at the nuns.

Leoba at once summoned her flock to discover which, if any, of the nuns was missing. Only Agatha was absent and she had had permission from Leoba to visit her parents. Agatha was at once recalled. She asserted her innocence and prayed that the true offender might be revealed. Leoba ordered the nuns to the chapel. The entire Psalter was recited by the nuns, with their arms outstretched, as our Lord's were upon the Cross. Prayers and processions followed. Then Leoba stood before the altar and stretched up her arms in supplication. "O Lord Jesus Christ," she prayed, "King of virgins, Lover of chastity, unconquerable God, manifest Thy power and deliver us from this charge, because the reproaches of those who reproached Thee have fallen upon us."

Leoba's prayers were heard, for soon after she had uttered them, the crippled girl confessed her crime and so saved the good name of the sisters.

This restoration of their reputation was regarded by all as a miracle, due to the merits and prayers of Leoba. Her biographer goes on to relate other miracles done by her: how with the help of some salt blessed by Boniface she put out a fire which threatened to destroy the village; how a violent storm abated when she called upon the name of Christ and made the sign of the cross; and how a nun was healed of haemorrhoids when Leoba fed her with milk from her own spoon.

So the fame of Leoba, abbess of Bischofsheim, spread from place to place. Men of influence and noble birth placed their daughters under her care and direction at the convent, and many widows left their homes and joined her community. All were attracted by her shining personality and her wonderful gifts of mind and spirit. Rudolph describes her as being "of angelic aspect, of pleasant speech, of clear intelligence, great in counsel, orthodox in faith, most patient in hope, most generous in charity."

Boniface, before engaging upon his last preaching mission to Frisia, sent for Leoba to advise and encourage her. She must not desert the land of her adoption, he said, nor tire of the work she had undertaken. Rather, she must endeavour to extend the scope of her work. "She must not count the spiritual life to be hard, nor the end difficult to attain, for the years of this life are short compared to eternity, and the sufferings of this world are as nothing in comparison with the glory that will be made manifest in the saints." Boniface then commended Leoba to the care of his successor, Lull, and to the senior monks of Fulda. He asked that her body, like his own, might be buried at Fulda so that "they who had served God during their lifetime with equal sincerity and zeal might await together the day of resurrection." Before leaving her, Boniface gave her his cowl and appealed to her once more not to forsake the land of her pilgrimage and not to be deterred by the thought of the years that lay ahead.

Leoba survived Boniface by about twenty-six years during which time she continued to govern the convent of nuns at Bischofsheim, and to found daughter houses. She extended the scope of her work, as Boniface had advised, and became a friend and counsellor of many. "The princes loved her, the nobles received her, the bishops welcomed her with joy." She was a well known and respected visitor at the court of Pippin whom Boniface had anointed king of the Franks. Her attachment to the court continued after Pippin's death when his son Charles the Great became king. Charles, we are told, frequently invited her to the court and loaded her with gifts for her religious houses. She was a friend of Charles' second wife, Hildegard, who wished dearly that she would leave her convent and come to reside at the court. Hildegard hoped in this way to have Leoba available at all times to benefit from her wise counsel. Leoba, however, disliked the pomp and splendour of court life and cared, above everything, for her work at the convents at Bischofsheim and its daughter houses.

Her visits to the monastery at Fulda were always welcomed by Lull and the senior monks, though normally no woman was allowed to cross the threshold of their house. Certain rules of propriety were always observed by Leoba. She would never enter the monastery alone and was accompanied by one of her older nuns. If other sisters had travelled with her they were left at a cell some distance from the monastery. Visits were only made by Leoba in daylight. When she arrived she would first spend some time in prayer. Then she would have talks with a few of the brethren, discussing, no doubt, the affairs of her convents and the work of the Church's mission among the heathen.

Leoba continued to administer her convent at Bischofsheim until she was too old to bear the responsibility any longer. Archbishop Lull advised her to resign the office of abbess and to retire quietly to one of the smaller daughter houses. She followed this advice and went to the house at Scoranesheim, a few miles south of Mainz. Her retirement was a short one, for not long after she arrived she fell sick and was confined to her bed. The priest, Torhthat, who for many years had been her private chaplain, ministered to her spiritual needs and brought her the Holy Sacrament. In the year 780 she died and "gave back her soul joyfully to her Creator."

Leoba's body was carried with great ceremony to the monastery at Fulda where it was interred in the same church as that of Boniface. It was reported that miracles of healing occurred there, due to the merits of Leoba and Boniface. Miraculous release was granted to a man bound with iron fetters and another recovered from a distressing disease which caused his limbs to twitch. So, even in death, these two saints, Leoba and Boniface, never failed to show the same compassion to the needy as they had done in their lifetime. The tomb of Leoba now stands in the crypt of the Church of St Petersberg in Fulda.

CHAPTER SEVEN

The West Saxon Mission to the Continent
Willibald, Bishop of Eichstatt

ONE OF the most charming and interesting of the *Saint's Lives* of this early period of English history is that of Willibald, a fellow worker of Boniface in Germany. A man of Wessex, he was at first attached to the monastery at Bishop's Waltham in Hampshire and later in life became bishop of Eichstatt in Bavaria. A further aspect of his life which is of particular interest is his remarkable and exhaustive tour of the Middle East and his visits to numerous shrines and holy places.

The author of the hagiography was an English nun, Hygeburg, who had also joined the German mission and become a member of the double monastery at Heidenheim, not far from Willibald's episcopal seat and monastery at Eichstatt. She refers with modesty to her attempt at writing a *Life of Willibald* and is sure that there were many priests who could do it better. She continues, "I, an unworthy sister of Saxon origin, last and least in life and manners, venture to write for the sake of posterity . . . a brief account of the early life of the venerable Willibald. Although I lack the experience and knowledge because I am but a weak woman, yet I would like, as far as lies in my power, to gather together a kind of nosegay of his virtues . . . * The work Hygeburg has written is, in fact, a unique piece of literature, not polished in style, but providing us with the first account of an Englishman's pilgrimage to the Holy Land and the holy places of the Middle East. Unlike the present day pilgrim's lightning tour of the Holy Land, lasting for a week or two, Willibald's tour, including a visit to Rome, covered a period of about ten years.

In her *Life of Willibald* Hygeburg gives us first a delightful account of the saint's childhood. He was born of devout West Saxon parents who cherished him exceedingly, all the more so because of

---

The Anglo-Saxon Missionaries in Germany. C. H. Talbot

his delicate health. At three years old he became seriously ill and seemed unlikely to recover. His parents, deeply distressed at the thought of losing their son and heir, took him into the fields and laid him at the foot of a stone cross, such as the Saxons were accustomed to erect in place of a church. Around such crosses clergy and people would meet for worship and individual believers came to offer their prayers. There, Willibald's parents prayed long and earnestly for the recovery of their son, promising that, in return for his life, they would offer him to serve God in a monastery.

To the joy of his parents the young Willibald recovered from his sickness. In obedience to their vow they entrusted him, several years later, to the care of the abbot Egwald, and the monks of the monastery at Bishop's Waltham in their own West Saxon kingdom. Under the guidance of his teachers he learned to read Latin, to study the texts of Scripture and to recite the Psalms. Many other studies were included in the curriculum of this and other monastic schools in England. Music, arithmetic, astronomy and ecclesiastical computation were among the subjects taught. Cosmography too, which dealt with the mapping of the world and the study of distant places of the earth, was a popular subject of study. Perhaps Willibald's enthusiasm for travel in general and for a pilgrimage to the holy places of the East in particular, arose from his study of books on cosmography. A book in circulation at the time, written by Adamnan, abbot of Iona, describing these holy places, was widely read in English monasteries. The material for the book was supplied to Adamnan by a French bishop, who had visited Iona on his return from a pilgrimage to the Holy Land. The finished book was presented by Adamnan to the King of Northumbria, Aldfrid. Aldfrid, a collector of books and a patron of the arts, realised the importance of the work and had copies of it made for general circulation. Copies no doubt reached many of the English monasteries, including those of Wessex, with which kingdom Alfrid was closely associated. It is of interest to find that both Adamnan and Hygeburg followed a similar method of writing and took down notes, almost by dictation it seems at times, from the travellers concerned, Adamnan from the French bishop, Arculf, and Hygeburg from Willibald. Had a copy of Adamnan's book reached the monastery at Heidenheim we may wonder or had Hygeburg seen it at her English convent, at Wimborne perhaps?

Apart from the influence of books on cosmography Willibald was living in an age of pilgrimage when it was the ambition of devout souls to kneel at the tombs of the Apostles in Rome or to go to some other holy place of pilgrimage. From Wessex went the two kings, Cadwalla and Ine, and two of the kingdom's most learned monks, Aldhelm and Boniface. Not only the great and famous went to Rome. Lesser folk, monks and nuns in great numbers joined the throngs of pilgrims to the Holy City. Boniface, in a letter to the archbishop of Canterbury, Cuthbert, expressed his dislike of the custom of women going to Rome on account of the moral dangers open to them. He writes:

"I will not conceal from your Grace that all the servants of God here, who are especially versed in Scripture and strong in the fear of God, are agreed that it would be well and favourable for the honour and purity of your Church, and a sure protection against vice, if your synod and your princes would forbid matrons and nuns to make their frequent journeys back and forth to Rome. A great part of them perish and few keep their virtue. There are many towns in Lombardy and Gaul where there is not a courtesan or a harlot but is of English stock. It is a scandal and disgrace to your whole Church."

Although the monasteries were the glory of England at this time, and through them the conversion of England was achieved and culture and learning advanced, yet there must have been monks and nuns ill-suited to the monastic life. Bede's account of the frivolous behaviour of the nuns at Coldingham who, instead of devoting themselves to prayer, study and useful labour, frittered away their time in gossip and fancy dressmaking, gives us a glimpse of what may have happened in some other religious establishments. There may well have been monks and nuns for whom a pilgrimage to Rome and the adventures of travel came as a welcome diversion from the dullness of life in a monastery with its strict routine and eternal round of daily offices.

But for earnest souls like Willibald a pilgrimage to Rome or the Holy Land was a religious exercise of great merit, an opportunity to grow in spiritual stature. At the age of about twenty "he began to devise means of setting out on pilgrimage and travelling to foreign countries unknown to him." He must have discussed his purpose with Abbot Egwald though Hygeburg does not say so. Instead she tells us that he confided in his father and used all his powers of persuasion to induce him to join him on his pilgrimage. We cannot admire the headstrong and enthusiastic young Willibald for insisting so vigorously that his father should accompany him; and, in view of future events, perhaps he felt some remorse at his insistence. At first his father stood his ground and refused to go with his son, saying that he could not leave his wife and children unprotected at home. But when Willibald continued with threats of damnation and promises of eternal life "softening his heart by describing the beauty of paradise and the sweetness of the love of Christ" he yielded to his son's entreaties. A brother, Wynnebald, and a number of friends were also coaxed into making the pilgrimage with Willibald.

In the summer of a year around 720 Willibald and his party sailed from Southampton Water across the Channel to France. They landed at the mouth of the Seine and made their way to the busy market town of Rouen where they stayed for a few days. They were in the Kingdom of the Franks, governed at that time by Charles Martel. Boniface had left England a few years earlier and was at work in Frisia with Archbishop Willibrord of Utrecht. It has been suggested that Boniface was perhaps related to Willibald. He seems to have had no hesitation in recommending him to the pope for work in the mission fields of Germany and later in ordaining him to a bishopric.

The party then crossed from France into Italy. The arduous journey must have been too much for Willibald's ageing father for when they reached Lucca, near Pisa, in northern Italy, he became fatally ill, his tired limbs growing stiff and cold. With filial devotion the two sons buried their father at a church in Lucca where he was later venerated as a saint.

They then continued their journey southwards towards Rome, gazing in rapture at the snow covered peaks of the Appenine mountains. In Rome they visited the shrines of the Apostles, St Peter and St Paul, and gave thanks for their escape from the perils of the journey. By now it was autumn and time to celebrate the feast of St Martin. With winter ahead, travel would be hazardous. It was a time when pilgrims and wayfarers abandoned their journeyings and waited for the spring. Willibald and his brother decided to stay in Rome for the winter and to devote themselves to prayer and fasting and the observance of their monastic rule. Winter passed and the warm days of spring approached. With the milder weather came an outbreak of plague in Rome. Both men fell victim to the disease and were racked with fever. They recovered, however, by the simple remedy of resting in turns; while one rested the other cared for his brother and ministered to his needs.

When they were quite restored to health Willibald was eager to continue his pilgrimage. He wished to visit the holy places of the Middle East where our Lord carried out his ministry and where the

Apostle Paul, and others, preached the Gospel. He must see the city of Jerusalem which, above all cities, stirred the longings and aspirations of pilgrims like Willibald. The way would be hard, the journey long, but like an athlete eager to try his strength, Willibald set out with two companions on this second stage of his pilgrimage. His brother, Wynnebald, did not accompany him, but stayed in Rome. It was some years before he was to see Willibald again. Other members of the party who had accompanied him from Britain also decided to remain in Rome and to offer up continual prayers for the safety of Willibald and his two friends.

Hygeburg gives a clear and detailed account of Willibald's wanderings all over the Middle East. Only occasionally do we find the pilgrims retracing their steps with what seems little reason. But considering the lack of proper maps and charts the journey is surprisingly orderly and the sequence of stopping places far from haphazard. Accurate observations are made which compare favourably with those made by modern travellers and descriptions are vivid and precise.

The journey is of great interest in itself and forms a major part of Hygeburg's *Life of Willibald*. Here it is only appropriate to give an outline of the journey which should provide the reader with an idea of the extent of Willibald's travels covering thousands of miles by land and sea. From Rome Willibald and his followers, who grew in numbers as the journey progressed, travelled south to Gaeta and from there by ship to Naples where they stayed for two weeks. Another ship took them to Reggio on the toe of Italy and across the Straits of Messina to Catania in Sicily. Catania was famous for the shrine of St Agatha to whom the local people prayed when threatened by eruptions from Mount Etna nearby. The party continued southwards to Syracuse and then took ship to Greece, Turkey and Cyprus, visiting all the places made famous by the apostle, Paul. From Cyprus they went across to Syria where Willibald and his companions, now numbering seven, faced hostile treatment from pagan Moors who suspected the pilgrims were spies. After a period of imprisonment their innocence was proved and they were freed.

The pilgrims now trudged southwards into Palestine and on to Jerusalem. But again they were suspected of spying and were imprisoned until the ruler of the province had ascertained their country of origin and the purpose of their journey. Assured that they were harmless the ruler released them; but Willibald fearing further hostility, left the city intending to return later. They turned northwards once more and came to Damascus, the scene of St Paul's conversion. When fear of hostility had died down they returned to Palestine visiting all the places associated with our Lord: among these were Cana, Capernaum, Nazareth, Tiberias. In the river Jordan at the traditional site of Christ's baptism, Willibald immersed himself in the water. The party then came again to Jerusalem and visited all the holy places in the city. While here Willibald fell ill and was confined to his bed for some weeks. When he had recovered he continued his tour of many more holy places including Bethlehem and the shepherd's field. Next they journeyed down to Gaza where for two months Willibald lost his sight. A third visit to Jerusalem brought about his recovery and the pilgrimage continued with visits to Caesarea, Sidon, Tripoli, Tyre, two more visits to Damascus and two more to Jerusalem. Finally the party boarded a ship at Tyre and after a voyage of about six months, presumably by way of the Mediterranean and the Aegean Seas, they came to Constantinople.

Here the restless wanderer came to a halt, remaining for two years in the city. The bodies of saints Andrew, Luke and Timothy rested in one of its churches and Willibald was granted an alcove near to their tombs where he could sit in quiet contemplation. Here too, he had time to reflect upon all the impressions of his protracted travels. But Willibald was still a young man of about thirty and his life's work lay ahead. He needed, he thought, more training in the monastic life; he had been barely twenty when he left the West Saxon monastery at Bishop's Waltham. He would go now to the monastery at Monte Cassino, the most famous in Europe and the home of the author of the Benedictine Rule. Benedict had founded the monastery there in the early years of the sixth century and formulated his "little rule for beginners", the importance of which he could never have known.

The company was now ready to leave Constantinople. They took a ship to Italy, landing at Reggio and after a visit to the island of Volcano they journeyed northwards to Monte Cassino, situated between Naples and Rome. At Monte Cassino Willibald and some of his companions were accepted by Abbot Petronax into the community of monks. Here Willibald learned much from his teachers and set himself the task of putting into practise the Rule of St Benedict in every detail. Those who had shared his travels received help and instruction from him; he himself became a model of monastic virtue. He showed his fellow monks "not so much by words as by the beauty of his character what was the real spirit of their institute." Willibald stayed at Monte Cassino for ten years, being appointed to various offices connected with the house. He was sacristan of the church and dean and porter of the monasteries.

When a Spanish priest arrived as a guest at Monte Cassino and wished to go to Rome the abbot chose Willibald to accompany him. News of Willibald's travels and of his holy life had now spread far and wide. The pope, Gregory III, had heard much of him from Boniface who had recently been in Rome. Boniface considered that Willibald would be a valuable recruit to the mission fields of Germany and asked the pope if he might be sent to join his team of workers. When Gregory heard that Willibald was in Rome he sent for him and questioned him on his travels in the Middle East. Willibald humbly recounted all the details of his journey and his visits to the shrines of the Saints and the holy places of Palestine. Gregory, impressed by all he heard, told Willibald that he wished to despatch him to Germany to work under Archbishop Boniface. Willibald replied that he was ready to go wherever the pope wished to send him.

Acting on the pope's orders Willibald returned to Monte Cassino and from there went to Germany. Boniface sent his new recruit to Eichstatt in Bavaria to assess the possibility of making the place a centre of missionary activity. Willibald found the area desolate and neglected. It had once been the scene of missionary activity, for there was a small church there dedicated to St Mary. This, he thought, could be used until a larger one could be built. He surveyed the ground and selected a suitable site for the building of a house for himself and his fellow workers. Then Willibald returned to Boniface at Freising to report on what he had found. Boniface ordained Willibald to the priesthood in preparation for his work at Eichstatt where he was to carry out a preaching mission to the inhabitants of the district.

At Eichstatt Willibald built a monastery and governed it on the lines of that at Monte Cassino, he and the monks observing the same Rule of St Benedict with additions from other monastic rules which he had seen observed during his travels. Many disciples were attracted to his monastery and were shown the path of perfection through obedience to the Rule. "Like a hen that cherishes her offspring beneath her wings, he won over many adoptive sons to the Lord, protecting them continually with the shield of his kindliness." Eventually this monastery with its new church became widely known as a place of culture, devotion and learning, and, as a retreat from the world, it became to Willibald what Fulda had been to Boniface and Echternacht to Willibrord.

At about this time, around 740, Boniface summoned Willibald to Thuringia to see his brother Wynnebald from whom he had parted some years earlier in Rome. After this meeting the two brothers were to see each other more often, for Wynnebald was made abbot of the double monastery at Heidenheim not many miles from Willibald's base at Eichstatt. This same double monastery was later to be governed by their sister, Walpurgis, who had been a nun at Wimborne Minster.

In 741 Willibald, now forty years old, was consecrated bishop of Eichstatt by Boniface. The consecration took place at Salzburg. For over forty years Willibald administered the see of Eichstatt devoting himself to evangelistic and pastoral work in Bavaria "driving the plough, sowing the divine seed and reaping the harvests, with the help of many labourers." He died in 786, an old man of about eighty-six.

It is of interest to find Willibald's name among a list of overseas bishops, headed by Boniface, who wrote to the English king, Aethelbald of Mercia, denouncing him for his lax morals. The letter was written in about 746 when Aethelbald had been reigning for thirty years and had become pre-eminent among the kings of the English. Bede speaks of him as overlord of the kingdoms south of the Humber. The power of Wessex had declined with the abdication of King Ine, history attaching little importance to the kings who immediately succeeded him. Boniface and his fellow bishops must have learned with dismay of the scandalous behaviour of the man who was now the dominant figure on the English political scene. They acknowledged the peacefulness of his reign and his liberality in almsgiving but deplored his violation of church privileges and his debauchery with women of the cloister. Even the pagans of Old Saxony had their rules of conduct in these matters and the Wends, depraved though they were, exalted marriage so highly that, after the death of her husband, it was considered praiseworthy for a woman to take her own life too. Did not Aethelbald recall that his predecessor, King Ceolred, became insane and died young as a result of his dissipated life, and the young King Osred of Northumbria likewise came to a bad end? "Wherefore, most dear son, beware of the pit into which you have seen others fall before you."*

Aethelbald's long reign of forty-one years, marred by tyranny and violence, was to end with his own violent death at the hands of a

_____

*English Historical Documents. Vol. 1 No. 177

member of his bodyguard. He was murdered in 757 at Seckington, near Tamworth. But he had lived long enough to hear of the martyrdom of the man who was responsible for that letter of stern rebuke. By the time Boniface died in 754, his native Wessex had become a mere satellite of Aethelbald's great Mercian kingdom. However depraved the latter years of his life, Aethelbald had restored Mercia to a place of pre-eminence among the English kingdoms which it had not known since the days of Penda. He had laid the foundation for the reign of a king who was to eclipse him in achievement, statesmanship and renown and in international reputation. This was Offa, king of Mercia and "the glory of Britain." At this point we turn from the history of Wessex to that of Mercia.

CHAPTER EIGHT

King Penda and the Early History of Mercia

MERCIA, the English kingdom of the Midlands, occupied, in its early history, the valley of the River Trent. Later, after military conquests, it covered a much wider area and included Middle Anglia, Lindsey and parts of Wessex. Its single dynasty, that of Penda, simplifies the study of its history. Penda dominates the political scene of early England, his aggressive militarism striking terror into the hearts of neighbouring kingdoms. Bede, in his *Ecclesiastical History,* presents him as the last survivor of an age of pagan Anglo-Saxon warriors. While all the other kings, one by one, surrender to the faith of the Christian missionaries, Penda resolutely opposes their teaching and clings to the pagan faith of his ancestors.

Bede first presents him to the reader as a warrior of the royal house of Mercia who had allied himself to Cadwallon, king of the Welsh, in a war against Northumbria. Their two armies devastated the kingdom, slaughtering her people, men, women and children, without mercy. The Northumbrian king, Edwin, died a martyr's death at their hands. He was succeeded by King Oswald, "a most Christian king" who, ten years later, met the same fate. Penda and his cruel Mercian warriors overran the Northumbrian kingdom spreading ruin far and wide, reaching the gates of the royal city of Bamborough and attempting to set it on fire.

We hear, too, of Penda's devastating attacks upon East Anglia, his forces killing King Sigbert, a reluctant warrior who had recently entered a monastery, possibly at Bury St Edmunds. In the same battle, his kinsman, Egric, who had succeeded to the kingdom, was mercilessly slain. Some years later King Anna, "an excellent man of royal stock, and father of a distinguished family" fell too in battle against Penda.

Wessex, as we have seen, was also subjected to attacks by Penda when her king, Cenwalh, offended the proud warrior. Cenwalh had put away his wife, who was a sister of King Penda, and re-married. The action was a slight against Penda; it must be repaid with retaliatory action. Penda immediately invaded Cenwalh's West Saxon kingdom and drove him out.

But of all Penda's neighbouring kingdoms, Northumbria bore the brunt of his aggression. Northumbria was Penda's greatest threat. Two of her kings, Edwin and Oswald, had held sway over all the kingdoms south of the Humber. Now the third, Oswy, the brother of Oswald, was likely, if not prevented, to succeed to the place of pre-eminence among the English kings. Mercian attacks therefore were made upon Northumbria, Penda declaring his intention of completely destroying the kingdom. In an attempt to appease Penda King Oswy offered him royal treasure and gifts of great worth, but all were refused. Oswy was forced to take up arms against Penda and, with his small army, to offer what resistance he could. Events turned out in his favour, Oswy and his son, Alchfrid, we are reminded, having God on their side. They perhaps also had the advantage of fighting on territory, near Leeds, which they knew well. Weather conditions favoured them too. They seem to have manoeuvred their forces so that the Mercian warriors were driven towards the flood waters. Heavy rains, Bede tells us, had recently caused the nearby river Winwaed to overflow and to flood the surrounding countryside. More of Penda's men perished, he says, by drowning, while trying to escape, than by the sword. Most of his thirty commanders were killed and Penda himself perished. The year was 655. Oswy now held the title of Bretwalda, overlord of the English, ruler of Britain. With the death of Penda the dark cloud over England had lifted.

As a Christian king, Oswy was concerned to encourage the advancement of his religion in the kingdoms of the English subject to his overlordship. He it was who, with well reasoned argument, persuaded his friend, King Sigbert of Essex, to accept Christianity and to invite preachers into his kingdom. The most notable of the preachers was Bishop Cedd, Apostle of Essex, who, before going into Essex had preached in Middle Anglia, a sub-kingdom of Mercia. Middle Anglia was roughly equivalent to the present day county of Leicestershire. It was to be the starting place of a Christian mission which was to spread throughout Mercia.

Middle Anglia was ruled by Penda's son, Peada, whom Bede describes as "a noble young man, well deserving the title and dignity of a king." He had married a princess of the royal house of Northumbria, a daughter of Oswy named Alchfled. The marriage had been conditional upon his acceptance of Christianity, the princess having already become a Christian. Peada therefore underwent a course of instruction. He was so impressed by the teaching he received that he declared his intention to accept the Christian Faith for its own sake even though he may never marry Alchfled. The marriage, however, took place and Peada became the son-in-law of King Oswy of Northumbria. He was now also the brother-in-law of King Alchfrid, sub-king of Deira, the southern part of the Northumbrian kingdom. King Alchfrid was a fervent Christian, a friend of Wilfrid and a keen supporter of the Roman Church. He, like his father Oswy, encouraged Peada to accept Christianity and to concern himself with the conversion of his people of Middle Anglia.

Until now we have presented the pagan king, Penda, in a wholly unfavourable light. Yet Bede points out one redeeming feature in his otherwise harsh character. He tells us that Penda, though not accepting Christianity himself, expected those who did to practise it sincerely. Those who despised the commandments of the God they professed to believe in were themselves only worthy of being despised. Furthermore, we are told that Penda did not forbid the preaching of the Christian Faith where there were people ready to listen, even if it were in Mercia itself. Perhaps it was this leniency towards Christian preachers which led the carvers of the statues on the west front of Lichfield cathedral to depict King Penda of Mercia clutching a cross. His indifference to Christianity and his lack of positive support to missionary preachers deterred any, however, from attempting to convert the kingdom.

Penda did not, it seems, attempt to prevent his son, Peada, from accepting Christian baptism nor from inviting preachers into Middle Anglia. These two events, together with Penda's marriage to Oswy's daughter, took place in about 653, two years before Penda's death in the battle of the Winwaed.

Peada was not alone in receiving instruction in the Faith. He was joined by his close companions, his thanes and their servants and all were baptized by the bishop of Lindisfarne, Finan. Following on this baptism, Peada wished to see the ordinary people of his realm converted too. Four priests were invited into Middle Anglia to conduct a preaching mission. Three were Englishmen, Cedd, Adda, and Betti; the fourth was Diuma, an Irishman. There was no lack of response to the preaching of these men. Bede says that every day many nobles and commoners came to hear them and to receive baptism.

But it was not until after the death of Penda that Christianity, which had made such strides in Middle Anglia, spread to Mercia itself, its advance encouraged by both Peada and his overlord, Oswy of Northumbria. A bishop was needed now to carry out the ordination of priests and to discharge other episcopal duties. Diuma was chosen and, as there was a shortage of clergy at this time, he was bishop of both Middle Anglia and Mercia. The *Anglo-Saxon Chronicle* records that after the death of his father, Penda, Peada succeeded to the kingdom of Mercia, though we must assume that a good deal of the control lay in the hands of Oswy. In any case Peada, whatever the extent of his power, did not rule for long. In the spring of 656 at Eastertide he was assassinated, through the treachery, it was thought, of his own wife. In regard to the authority exercised by Peada and the power which remained in the hands of Oswy, Bede's account differs from the *Anglo-Saxon Chronicle*, in that he states that Oswy gave Peada only the part of Mercia, south of the Trent, to govern.

If we are to believe the *Anglo-Saxon Chronicle* (E), and there seems no good reason why we should doubt the authenticity of the account (though the bare facts may have been expanded and certain legendary elements included), it was Peada and Oswy who were responsble for the founding of a monastery at Peterborough, then known as Medeshamstede. Bede too refers to the monastery when he tells how the abbot, Sexwulf, was subsequently appointed bishop of Mercia. The *Anglo-Saxon Chronicle* gives a detailed account of its establishment, the charters pertaining to it, its consecration, endowment and so on which we can only give here in outline.

The monastery, built in about 654, was first ruled by Abbot Sexwulf, to whom the *Chronicle* refers as "a great friend of God, and all people loved him, and he was very nobly born in the world and powerful." After King Peada's death, when his brother Wulfhere ruled Mercia, the monastery acquired great wealth. Under the supervision of Sexwulf, the building was completed and endowed by King Wulfhere with estates and property, gold and silver and everything else necessary. Then the monastery was consecrated by the archbishop of Canterbury, Deusdedit, in the presence of the king, his brother Ethelred, his sisters Cyneburh and Cyneswith and all the thanes in his kingdom. Several bishops helped with the service of consecration: Ithamar of Rochester, Wini of London, Jaruman of Mercia and Tuda, later of Lindisfarne. Wilfrid, then still only a priest, was there too; with his love of ecclesiastical ritual and ceremony how he must have delighted in the occasion. After the consecration King Wulfhere read out a list of lands and waters, meres, fens and weirs which he was giving to the abbot and monks of the monastery, the charter being witnessed and signed by many notable clergy and earldormen. This consecration ceremony reminds us of that held some years later at Ripon when Wilfrid, now a bishop, read out a list of lands at Catlow, Dent, Ribble, Yeadon and other places given to him by royal patrons.*

Peterborough became one of the most important centres of religious devotion, learning and evangelism in the Midlands. Daughter houses soon sprang up in other parts of Mercia and beyond, administered by monks from Peterborough who were answerable to its abbot. Such daughter houses were founded at Breedon-on-the-Hill in Leicestershire, now renowed for its beautiful frieze of Saxon carvings, Brixworth in Northamptonshire, Woking and Bermondsey in Surrey, Hoo in Kent and probably others unrecorded. Bede tells us that it was from the monastery of Breedon that one of the archbishops of Canterbury came. He was Tatwini, "a man distinguished for his religion and wisdom and extremely learned in Holy scripture." He was the ninth archbishop of Canterbury (731-734). Is this the same Tatwini, perhaps, who years before, as a young man and native of the fens, escorted the anchorite, Guthlac, in a boat to the remote and lonely island of Crowland where Guthlac was to live a very holy and austere life?

A particularly interesting church survives at Brixworth, much of it dating from the seventh century. It incorporates some Roman masonry, suggesting the importance of this hill site in Roman times with its commanding view of the surrounding countryside. Although now lacking some of its original structure, its side aisles and porticos, two western porches, original apse and possibly a crypt below it, give a good idea of how magnificent a church it was when first built. Its size suggests the existence of a thriving religious community of monks, its large church affording ample space for local worshippers who were accustomed to use monastic churches.

We know, through occasional references in contemporary literature, of the existence of other monastic centres in Mercia. In Felix's *Life of Guthlac* we are told that, after abandoning a military career, Guthlac joined a double monastery at Repton where the monks and nuns were ruled by the Abbess Aelfthryth. We know nothing of the founding of the monastery. It is not unlikely that Wilfrid had some connection with it. Eddius, in his *Life of Wilfrid*, relates how King Wulfhere of Mercia frequently invited Wilfrid into his kingdom to

---

Life of Wilfrid. Eddius Ch. 17

carry out episcopal duties and gave him numerous estates for the founding of the monasteries. Some years later and shortly before his death, Wilfrid made a tour of his monasteries in Mercia and was received joyfully by their various abbots. Eddius tells how "every community was provided for according to its needs; some got grants of land to increase their revenues, the rest were left a legacy." When the tour was over he came to his monastery at Oundle in Middle Anglia where he had earlier dedicated a church to St Andrew. Here at Oundle he died, his body later being transferred to Ripon where he was buried.

The king of Mercia during Wilfrid's last years was Ceolred. There is perhaps an underlying reason for Eddius' statement that Wilfrid had, upon the request of two of his abbots, agreed to go and confer with King Ceolred "for the sake of the monasteries we have in that kingdom". Ceolred was a notorious troublemaker in his dealings with the monasteries up and down the country, disregarding their rights and privileges and seducing young nuns dedicated to God. If there is any truth in Eddius' claim that Ceolred wished to make Wilfrid his spiritual director and to follow the advice he gave in regulating his life, his good intention was shortlived. Boniface tells how he went out of his mind and died young while feasting with his companions "without repentance and confession, raging and distracted, conversing with devils and cursing the priests of God."* The conception of Heaven and Hell was strong in early Christian teaching and the literature surrounding it abundant. A monk of Wenlock claimed to have seen a vision, in which King Ceolred appeared suffering torments in Hell, as a punishment for his evil life. The vision is described by Boniface in a letter to an English nun.

Monasticism, then, flourished in Mercia under King Wulfhere, successor of Peada. Wulfhere had risen to power with the help of a few faithful earldormen who had kept him hidden while they plotted a rebellion against King Oswy of Northumbria whose officers ruled Mercia following the death of Penda. They drove out the officers from Mercia, recovered the land they had lost and proclaimed as their king this young son of Penda, Wulfhere. If one pieces together the scattered references to him from Bede's *History*, Eddius' *Life of Wilfrid* and a contemporary charter, a picture emerges of a king powerful enough to merit the honoured title of Bretwalda, Ruler of Britain, though he is not so named among Bede's list of early Bretwaldas. He ruled from 657 to 674. In 661 we

---

English Historical Documents. No. 177

find him, according to the *Anglo-Saxon Chronicle*, in West Saxon territory, harrying as far as the Berkshire Downs and further south gaining a conquest of the Isle of Wight. The latter he gave to his friend and godson, King Ethelwalh of Sussex, together with the province of Meonware in eastern Hampshire. A charter of the time states that Wulfhere had a residence at Thame, to the east of Oxford, indicating his occupation of this part of Wessex. His overlordship of Essex in about 664 is certain since Bede tells us that the two kings of these people, Sighere and Sebbi, were subject to him. At about the same time London, an international trading centre and chief city of the East Saxons, came under Wulfhere's control giving him also authority over its bishopric. When this fell vacant he was in a position to fill it with a man of his own choice. Wini, recently expelled from the West Saxon see, took refuge in Wulfhere's kingdom and offered him money for the see of London. To this illegal proposition Wulfhere agreed and Wini was made bishop of London.

Between 671 and 675 Wulfhere attempted by force of arms to bring under his yoke the great kingdom of Northumbria, ruled then by King Egfrid. But the attack failed. Wulfhere was defeated by Egfrid, lost control of the kingdom of Lindsey and found his own kingdom of Mercia subject to Northumbria. Eddius describes the episode thus: "Now Wulfhere, king of the Mercians, proud of heart and insatiable in spirit, roused all the southern nations against our kingdom . . . So Egfrid, with a band of men no greater than theirs, attacked a proud enemy, and by the help of God overthrew them with his tiny force. Countless numbers were slain, the king was put to flight and his kingdom laid under tribute . . . "

Against this political background we must now review the religious scene in Mercia. We have seen that the first bishop of Middle Anglia and Mercia was Diuma. But both his own, and his successor's, Ceollach's, episcopate were short. Their successor appointed in King Wulfhere's reign was Trumhere, an Englishman, though he had been consecrated by Celtic bishops. Trumhere had been abbot of the monastery at Gilling and was related to the royal family of Northumbria. He was appointed to the bishopric of Mercia in about 659 soon after Wulfhere had come to power. He was to govern the Church until 662. Trumhere was succeeded by Jaruman who was bishop of the Mercians from 662 to 667. Bede tells us little about his activities in Mercia itself but describes how he helped to re-convert the East Saxons who, at the time, were subject to King Wulfhere. Part of their kingdom was ruled by an apostate king, Sighere, who during an outbreak of plague, relapsed into paganism and the worship of idols. Wulfhere, their overlord, concerned at this rejection of the Christian Faith which they had once accepted, sent Bishop Jaruman from Mercia into Essex to correct their error. Jaruman, "a religious and good man" travelled widely over the Essex countryside preaching to the people of that kingdom and recalling them to the true Faith once more.

After the death of Jaruman in 667 there seemed no obvious successor to fill the bishopric of Mercia. It is to this period, between about 666 and 669, that we should assign the visits of Bishop Wilfrid to Mercia from his monastery at Ripon, to fulfil episcopal duties at the request of King Wulfhere. The year 669 saw the arrival in Canterbury of a new archbishop, the scholarly and statesmanlike Theodore who lost no time in visiting every part of Britain and reorganising the English Church, increasing the number of bishoprics. He filled the bishopric of Mercia by consecrating Chad, "a holy man, modest in his ways, learned in the Scriptures, and careful to practise all that he found in them."

CHAPTER NINE

St Chad, Apostle of Mercia

CHAD was a member of a distinguished family of churchmen. The most famous of his brothers was Cedd, preacher to the Middle Angles in the kingdom of Mercia, founder and abbot of a monastery at Lastingham in Northumbria's southern kingdom of Deira, and bishop of the East Saxons in the area which is now Essex. A second brother, Cynibil, was a priest and helped Cedd in his preparations for the founding of the monastery at Lastingham. A third brother, Caelin, also a priest, was chaplain to the sub-king of Deira, Ethelwald, administering the Word and Sacraments to the king and his family. It was King Ethelwald who donated the estate to Cedd for the founding of Lastingham monastery.

As a young man Chad had joined the throng of Englishmen who went to Ireland to study under the learned Celtic monks. One of his fellow Englishmen was Egbert who wished to become an exile in Ireland for the love of Christ and for the atonement of his sins. He it was who played an important part in initiating the English mission to the Continent. While Egbert stayed in Ireland for the rest of his life, Chad returned to England and became abbot of the monastery at Lastingham, succeeding his brother Cedd.

Oswy, the king of Northumbria at that time, had a high regard for Chad and, because of the inconvenience caused by the absence of his newly appointed bishop, Wilfrid, he appointed Chad to fill the temporary vacancy and to perform episcopal functions in Northumbria. Possibly too, Oswy was glad to take this opportunity of appointing a bishop of his own choice, Wilfrid having been nominated by his son Alchfrid. There was a dearth of bishops in England at the time and the archbishopric of Canterbury itself was vacant since Deusdedit had recently died and no successor had been appointed. Chad's consecration to the bishopric, for reasons not quite certain, was irregular and uncanonical, probably because two Celtic bishops were called in to assist Bishop Wini of the West Saxon diocese in the consecration ceremony.

Chad, however, took up his appointment as bishop of York in 666 and ruled the diocese very ably until 669. He preached the Faith in cities and towns and in country districts, always walking from place to place as his master Bishop Aidan had done, in imitation of the Apostles, and as his own brother Cedd had done before him. In his methods of instruction he imitated Aidan also, endeavouring to maintain the truth and purity of the Church, and in his personal life devoting himself to the practice of humility and temperance. There must have been many northerners who regretted the departure of Chad, their bishop, when Wilfrid was reinstated by the new archbishop of Canterbury, Theodore, in 669. In the pages of Bede and Eddius, Wilfrid emerges as a figure of great distinction, dominating the scene of English church life in the second half of the seventh century, yet he lacks the gentle nature and homeliness which so endeared Chad to his flock.

Though Chad was deposed from his episcopal office in the north, Theodore was well aware of his ability and the goodness of his character. Such a man should continue to serve the Church as a bishop, thought Theodore. He therefore informed Chad that there was no need for him to lose his episcopal status though he must be reconsecrated according to catholic rites. To this Chad humbly agreed and whatever had been lacking in his early consecration was now made good by Theodore. With Wilfrid in office at York, Chad returned to his quiet life as abbot of Lastingham, though not for long.

When the bishopric of Mercia became vacant after the death of Jaruman, and Wilfrid, who had carried out some episcopal duties for King Wulfhere, had returned to the north, Theodore suggested that the king should accept Chad as the new bishop of Mercia together with the province of Lindsey. To this the king agreed; but the appointment had also to be sanctioned by the king of Northumbria, Oswy, because Chad was a subject of that kingdom. Oswy agreed to the appointment and in 669 Chad became bishop of Mercia and Lindsey. In the latter kingdom King Wulfhere gave Chad fifty hides of land at Barrow-on-Humber for the establishment of a monastery.

In Mercia itself Chad's episcopal seat was at Lichfield which, according to Eddius' *Life of Wilfrid*, had originally been given to Wilfrid. Eddius describes it as "a place highly suitable for an episcopal see either for himself or anyone he might choose to give it to." It is almost certain that Wilfrid, with his passion for building monasteries, would have erected one on this large and important estate. When Chad was appointed to the bishopric and installed at Lichfield we can assume that a church and monastery already existed there for his use. Being a monk as well as a bishop he would have shared the community life of the monastery, the church becoming his cathedral. Bede tells us that he also built himself a private house not far from the monastery and church, to which he could retire for periods of quiet, when he would occupy himself in prayer and study. Sometimes seven or eight of the brethren would join him there. One of his closest companions was the monk, Owini, who had been attached to his monastery at Lastingham and was at one time chief steward to the East Anglian princess, Etheldreda. Owini was a practical rather than as studious man and when the others were engrossed in study he would find some task to perform outside.

Eddius describes Bishop Chad as "an extremely meek man and a true servant of God." Bede tells us that Archbishop Theodore persuaded him to forsake his cherished custom of travelling everywhere on foot, especially when he was compelled to cover great distances in the performances of his duties as a bishop. To encourage him Theodore, on one occasion, even helped to lift him onto his horse.

Bede gathered a great amount of information about Chad from the monks of Lastingham and from one monk in particular. This was Trumbert who had been trained under Chad but later moved to the monastery at Jarrow where Bede was a pupil. From Trumbert Bede received instruction in the Scriptures. He once told Bede that Chad was so mindful of the approach of death that at times of inclement weather he would lay aside his work and implore God's mercy for mankind, especially in time of gales and violent storms. Then he would prostrate himself on the ground and pray most earnestly, or go to the church and devote his mind to psalms and prayers until the storms had passed. When asked by the monks why he did this he would reply that God sent lightning and thunder "to move the inhabitants of the earth to fear him, and to remind them of the judement to come . . . therefore we should respond to his heavenly warnings with the fear and love we owe him."

Chad was bishop of Lichfield for only two and a half years. On 2nd March 672 he died of plague and was buried in his cathedral church of St Mary at Lichfield. Wonderful manifestations surround his passing. Bede relates how, shortly before his death, his faithful friend Owini was working in the grounds outside the bishop's house when he heard singing of surpassing sweetness coming, it seemed from heaven itself and descending over the oratory where Chad was at prayer. Owini listened with rapt attention for perhaps half an hour. Then the singing died away and returned from whence it came. As Owini stood wondering what could be the meaning of this heavenly sign Chad threw open the window and clapped his hands, as was his custom when he wished to draw anyone's attention. At once Owini answered his call and hurried inside. He was to go to the church, said Chad, and bring back the seven companions who were accustomed to share his hours of prayer. Owini went at once and brought back the brethren. When they arrived Chad gathered them round him and addressed them with a note of urgency in his voice. They must continue in love and peace with each other and faithfully obey the monastic rule which he had taught them. He said he had received a forewarning of his death. Therefore they must return to the church and commend his passing to the Lord and let each one of them prepare for his own passing by vigils and prayers and good deeds "for no man knows the hour of his death."

Then the sorrowing companions returned to the church to pray for their master. Only then did Owini dare to ask the bishop what was the meaning of the joyous singing he had heard over the oratory. Chad told him, in confidence, that the angels had come to warn him of his approaching death and would return in seven days to take his soul to heaven where he would share the joys of the Blessed which he had so much hoped and longed for. Owini must tell no man of what had occurred until after Chad's death. Soon Chad fell victim to the plague, as did many other monks, and as the days passed he grew steadily weaker. After receiving the Sacrament of Christ's Body and Blood, he died. At first he was buried in the church of St Mary in Lichfield. Later when the new church of St Peter was built, occupying the same site as the present cathedral, his bones were translated to that place by Bishop Headda. Egbert, Chad's friend and companion in Ireland, told how a man — probably himself — saw, in a vision at the time of Chad's death the soul of Chad's brother Cedd, who had died some years before, descending from heaven with hosts of angels, to take Chad to the heavenly abode. However fanciful the vision may seem to present day sceptics it expresses the Christian belief in the immortality of the soul and of the continued involvement of the souls of the dead in the affairs of the living. The idea is particularly attractive to Bede who tells of similar manifestations accompanying the passing of St Hilda and St Cuthbert.

After Chad's death and while Wulfhere still governed the kingdom of Mercia, Bishop Wynfrith, "a good and modest man", who had been one of Chad's clergy, was appointed to administer the diocese of Mercia which still incorporated the provinces of Middle

Anglia and Lindsey. At the outset of his episcopate he was present at the first ecclesiastical council involving the entire English Church convened in 672 by Theodore at Hertford. A variety of matters were discussed and formal assent given by the clergy to ancient decrees of the Church. The latter included the decrees drawn up at the Council of Chalcedon concerning, among other things, the doctrine of the Person of Christ, his divine and human nature. The council at Hertford agreed too on the observing of Easter according to Roman rites and customs: bishops were not to intrude into the dioceses of others; monasteries were to be exempt from episcopal interference and from expropriation of their property; monks were to obey their abbots and not to wander off to other monasteries without dismissory letters; bishops and priests were forbidden to exercise their priestly functions in other dioceses without the permission of the resident bishop; bishops were not to clamour for precedence over others but were to yield to the seniority of their fellow bishops; synods were eventually to be held twice a year, though once a year at Clofeshoch in the first instance; more bishops were to be consecrated as the number of the faithful increased. Finally Christian standards of marriage were to be upheld.

A few years after this council, probably in 675, Wynfrith, bishop of Mercia was deposed from his bishopric through some act of disobedience, says Bede, which displeased Archbishop Theodore. It seems likely that this "act of disobedience" was connected with some clause or other of the Council's decisions upon which Wynfrith disagreed. It has been suggested that, like Wilfrid of York, he objected to the division of his diocese and the appointment of additional bishops to administer the extra sees. Wilfrid's Northumbrian see had not yet been divided but it is clear that it was scheduled for division in accordance with Theodore's policy on this question. But whatever the cause of Wynfrith's deposition, Bede tells us that he retired to his monastery at Barrow-on-Humber and lived a most holy life until his death. Eddius gives the additional piece of information that he travelled to the Continent at about the same time as Wilfrid, that is in 678, and was ill-treated at the hands of Ebroin, Mayor of the Palace under King Theodoric. This was owing to the similarity in the two prelates' names; the ill-treatment had really been intended for Wilfrid.

CHAPTER TEN

Further Developments in Mercia

AFTER King Wulfhere's death in 675 his brother, Ethelred, succeeded to the Mercian kingdom, ruling until 704. He seems, at first, to have been a warlike king with political and territorial ambitions. In 676, with an army no less powerful than that of his father Penda, he invaded Kent, "profaning churches and monasteries without fear of God or respect for religion." Among those places destroyed was the city of Rochester with its cathedral. The bishop, Putta, was away from the city at the time, but when he returned and saw the devastation of the city, the destruction of his church and the loss of all its treasures, he sought refuge with his friend Sexwulf, bishop of Mercia. It appears that he had no hope of recovering his see of Rochester and accepted from Sexwulf a church and a small estate in Mercia where he could live quietly as an ordinary priest. He had, however, a great interest in and knowledge of church music and Roman chant and travelled about the country whenever he was invited to give instruction at other monasteries. The see of Rochester survived but the destruction of its church and property left it greatly impoverished and the bishop whom Theodore consecrated in Putta's place, Cuichelm, held the office for only a short time. He was evidently not content to occupy a see so deprived, and was not energetic enough to revitalise it, so he resigned and went elsewhere. Theodore then consecrated Gebmund, but of him Bede tells us nothing. His more distinguished successor was Tobias, a man of wide learning who had been educated at Theodore's school at Canterbury acquiring such a thorough knowledge of Greek and Latin that, it is said, he knew the languages as well as his own Saxon tongue.

Several years after ravaging Kent, King Ethelred turned his attention towards Northumbria which throughout England's early history had been a target of Mercian invasion. We have seen that Ethelred's predecessor, Wulfhere, had attacked Northumbria and been defeated by King Egfrid, losing his hold over the kingdom of Lindsey and bringing his own kingdom of Mercia under the overlordship of Northumbria. Hostility, now in Ethelred's reign, broke out once more between the two kingdoms, Ethelred desiring to regain independence for Mercia and recovery of Lindsey. A battle was fought between the two armies near the river Trent in 679. A decisive victory was won by Ethelred who regained Lindsey and brought to an end Mercia's subjection to Northumbria.

But the peace between the two kingdoms was an uneasy one, since Ethelred's warriors had slain King Egfrid's young brother Elfwin, sub-king of Deira and the idol of all Northumbria. Eddius in his biography of Wilfrid tells us that when Elfwin's body was carried into York "the whole population wept and tore their hair for grief and rent their garments." But not only was Northumbria stunned by the loss of this popular young king; Mercia mourned the loss too, for Mercia's queen, Osthryth, was Elfwin's sister. As a consequence, hostility still smouldered between the two kingdoms, threatening to break out once more into violence. The peacemaker was Theodore, archbishop of Canterbury who by his wise advice "smothered the flames of this awful peril." Peace was restored between the two kings and their peoples. Compensation however, had to be paid, according to custom, by those responsible for the killing to the family of the slain. Ethelred of Mercia thus had to pay the appropriate sum of money, the worth of a king (the wergild, which differed according to the social status of the one who had been killed) to Egfrid of Northumbria for the death of his brother, Elfwin. For the present the feud had been settled without further bloodshed. One wonders, however, whether the murder of Queen Osthryth some eighteen years later in 697, by some Mercian noblemen, had any connection with her national origin and the age-old rivalry between Mercia and Northumbria.

Bede was about seven years old when the Battle of the Trent was fought. Years later when he was collecting material for his *Ecclesiastical History* he was told the story of one of the Northumbrian warriors who had taken part in the battle. This was Imma, a Northumbrian thane, who was seriously wounded and lay on the battlefield among the dead for many hours after fighting had ceased. Eventually Imma recovered consciousness, bandaged his wounds as best he could and went to look for help, hoping to find friends. But being unable to make a quick escape he fell into the hands of enemy soldiers who took him to their commander, a man of noble birth in the service of King Ethelred. Being afraid to reveal his true identity in case he should lose his life, Imma told the Mercian commander that he was a simple peasant who was accustomed to bring food to the army. The commander ordered

him to be given shelter and his wounds tended. When Imma
recovered, the commander, fearing that he might escape, ordered
him to be chained; but, through some mysterious power, whenever
he was chained, the chains fell from him. Soon it became apparent
to his captors that this man was no peasant; his appearance, dress
and speech confirmed his noble origin. Questioned by the commander, Imma confessed to being a king's thane. The commander,
because of a promise he had made to him, spared his life and sold
him to a Frisian slave-owner in London. Again the fetters that were
put upon him fell loose. Eventually the Frisian agreed to free him if
he could raise the money for his own ransom. He obtained this from
Hlothere, king of Kent, since he had once be a thane of Queen
Etheldreda of Northumbria whose sister, Sexburg, had married into
the royal house of Kent. Imma had always believed that the reason
for his chains repeatedly being loosened was that his brother,
Tunna, a priest in Northumbria, was praying and saying Masses for
him. Now that Imma was a free man he went to visit his brother who
confirmed that this was so; he had offered many prayers and Masses
for him at the hour of Terce and at that same hour Imma's chains
had been loosened. Many who heard Imma recount this story of how
he was helped by his brother's prayers were inspired to a deeper
faith in God and a firmer attention to their own prayers and
participation in the Mass.

The victory of King Ethelred in the battle of the Trent had freed
him from the Northumbrian yoke and given him authority over the
kingdom of Lindsey. Charters of the period confirm, too, his
authority south of the Thames. His name is associated with the
monastery at Abingdon in Berkshire and in 681 he made grants of
land to Aldhelm, abbot of Malmesbury, in south Gloucestershire
and north Wiltshire, and in 685 confirmed a grant of land at
Somerford Keynes, south of Cirencester.*

About this time also, the end of the seventh century, a religious
house was founded at Much Wenlock on the far western side of the
Mercian kingdom. Now in the county of Shropshire, Wenlock then
belonged to the sub-kingdom of Mercia, Magonsaete. It had once
been an independent kingdom and governed by its own local
dynasty, as is attested by the consistency of the alliteration of its
nomenclature, many of the names associated with it beginning with
the letter M. Later, probably during Penda's reign, it became a
dependent province of Mercia. The king of the Magonsaete was

*Anglo-Saxon England. F. Stenton. P. 68

Merewalh. He married a lady of the royal house of Kent and had a family of at least three daughters and a son. Of the daughters, Mildred became abbess of the minster in Thanet, Mildgyth was a nun at Eastry in Kent and Mildburg was abbess of Much Wenlock. As with all the seventh and eighth century minsters the founders had an eye to the beauty of the surroundings in which the houses were built. Either they were situated on glorious coastal sites, as at Coldingham, Folkestone and Whitby or in the heart of beautiful countryside. Much Wenlock was no exception. The minster was built on the north eastern edge of Wenlock Edge with commanding views of the surrounding hills, wooded slopes and sweeping valleys. The minster was evidently a double house as Boniface described a vision of one of the monks belonging to it. Two centuries after its foundation, the minster was destroyed by Danish invaders. It was revived by the Normans and given over to Cluniac monks. The extensive ruins which survive show what a large and splendid monastery this was.

The friendship and patronage which King Wulfhere had shown towards Wilfrid, bishop of York, was continued by King Ethelred. Eddius, in his *Life of Wilfrid*, describes the many trials endured by Wilfrid at the hands of the king of Northumbria, Egfrid, who drove him from his bishopric and confiscated many of his monasteries and estates including a number in Mercia. Later when the wrongs done to him had be redressed, the archbishop of Canterbury, Theodore, wrote to King Ethelred asking him to renew friendly relations with Wilfrid: "I urge you, beloved son, and charge you by the love of Christ, to do your utmost, as long as you live, to help this devoted servant of God, as you always used to in time past." Ethelred, as a result, treated Wilfrid with great respect and remained his faithful friend, in the future, returning many of his Mercian monasteries and estates. One wonders whether King Ethelred's decision to renounce the throne of Mercia and to enter a monastery was due in part to the persuasive influence of Wilfrid.

In the kingdom of Lindsey there was a monastery at Bardney which, says Bede, "was greatly loved, favoured and enriched by the queen and her husband Ethelred." The reason for their attachment to the monastery was that the remains of the Queen's uncle, Oswald, were buried there and Oswald had been a king of great distinction, ruling the kingdom of Northumbria wisely and setting an example of Christian devotion to all his people. When he fell in battle against the pagan King Penda of Mercia all acclaimed him as a martyr and his virtues were extolled at home and abroad. In Bardney Abbey his bones were placed in a casket over which was hung his royal banner of gold and purple. Many miracles of healing took place at Bardney and many pilgrims came to pray at Oswald's tomb. It was to this monastery that King Ethelred retired to become a monk in 704, about seven years after his wife's murder by Mercian nobles. Subsequently he became abbot of the monastery.

Ethelred's abdication brought to the throne of Mercia his nephew, Coenred, son of Wulfhere. We know nothing of political events in Mercia during his reign and even the *Anglo-Saxon Chronicle* is silent about the years between 704 and 709 which covered his short reign. Bede says only that he ruled with great renown. Bede does, however, relate in detail Coenred's efforts to reform one of his army commanders who, though he was a man of military distinction and served the king faithfully, was lax in his private life. He disregarded the king's advice that he ought to reform his ways saying that he would do so at a later date. Then illness struck him down and racked his body with dreadful pains. Again the king implored him to repent of his past misdeeds before death robbed him of the power to do so. But fearing to lose face in the eyes of his friends he promised to confess his sins when he recovered from his illness. As his illness worsened and he seemed unlikely to recover he fell into a state of despair and became the victim of horrible nightmares. He related to the king a vision he had had of his future damnation. A handsome youth appeared before him, holding a beautiful, but very small, book in which were written the few good deeds he had done in his past life. Then appeared a host of evil spirits bringing with them a book of great size in which were recorded all his sins of thought, speech and action. "This man belongs to us," said one of the evil spirits. "You are right," said the handsome youth, "take him and let him be joined to the company of the damned." And they took him and struck him with their tridents. Soon after his vision the man died, unrepentant and unforgiven; his vision, says Bede , being granted to him for the benefit of others rather than for himself, "in order that we should remember that our actions and thoughts are not scattered by the wind, but are all preserved to be examined by the Supreme Judge." Bede heard this story, he says, from the venerable Bishop Pecthelm, first English bishop of Whithorn in Galloway. Pecthelm had been trained under Aldhelm at Malmesbury and had corresponded with Boniface on the question of the permissible degrees of marriage within a family.

In 709 Coenred renounced the throne of Mercia, went to Rome and became a monk, spending the rest of his life "in prayer, fasting and acts of mercy." In early England the task of kingship, it seems, sometimes might take second place to a call to enter the cloister. This enthusiasm for monastic life must have sprung from the teaching and example of the first Christian missionaries, almost all of whom were themselves in religious orders. Thus we see in Bede's *Ecclesiastical History* that the call of the cloister took precedence over the fulfilment of royal office. Kings relinquished their crowns to become monks, and queens deserted their husbands to become nuns and abbesses. Coenred, says Bede, "resigned his kingly sceptre for a yet more noble kingdom." In the light of our knowledge of his successor Ceolred, we might think it better if he had continued to rule the kingdom of Mercia instead of becoming a monk. Ceolred, son of Ethelred, after a life of dissipation, died young and out of his mind. Ceolred was the last of Penda's descendents to rule Mercia and, with his death in 716, says Sir Frank Stenton, the first phase of Mercian history ends.

The Anglo-Saxon Missionaries to the Continent before Boniface

BEFORE Boniface's mission to the Germans, from 718 to 754, other Englishmen had gone over to the Continent to spread their faith. Among these were Wilfrid, Wictbert, Willibrord and Swidbert, all of whom were natives of Northumbria. Two other English priests, the Hewalds, possibly also Northumbrians, went to Old Saxony but were murdered before their mission could bear fruit. Nor should we forget the man who, though he never worked as a missionary on the Continent himself, was the inspiration behind the enterprise undertaken by others. He was Bishop Egbert, a saintly man, greatly admired by Bede and featuring prominently in his *Ecclesiastical History*.

The impulse which these Englishmen felt towards the mission fields of Europe may be attributed to a variety of causes. As with all missionary enterprise they were instilled with a desire to obey Christ's command to preach to all nations. The nations which demanded their attention, above all others, were those with whom they shared consanguinity, the Saxon race of the Continent. They were influenced too by the zeal of the Celtic Church which sent over to Europe a succession of missionary monks from Ireland. But it was not only the Celtic Christians who were enthusiastic missionaries. Rome too was imbued with the same spirit. It was Gregory the Great, pontiff of Rome, who sent over to Britain a band of missionary monks, led by Augustine, to convert the pagan Saxons. To the initiative of Rome we owe our conversion. Englishmen of the seventh and eighth centuries must have been deeply conscious of the debt they owed to Rome. Christians of the Roman party, like Wilfrid of York, followed in the same tradition. He was responsible for the conversion of Sussex, preached in almost every kingdom in England, administered the Church in Northumbria and was the first Englishman to transmit the faith to the pagans of Frisia in northern Europe.

Wilfrid arrived in Frisia in 678 on his way to Rome. Because it was then late summer or early autumn, and travel across Europe in winter was dangerous, he decided to winter in Frisia. Wilfrid gained the support of the king, Aldgils, and was given permission to preach to his people. Most of the chieftains and multitudes of commoners were baptised. The harvest that year was extremely abundant, which pleased the natives and made them take kindly to Wilfrid's preaching. His successful, though brief, mission had laid the foundation for the work of others, in particular that of Willibrord, his pupil at Ripon Minster.

Among the missionary enthusiasts of the late seventh century was Bishop Egbert, a Northumbrian, who had spent many years in voluntary exile in Ireland. Bede says of him that he lived a life of great humility, gentleness and simplicity and brought much blessing to his own people and those among whom he lived in Ireland. He had a longing too, to preach the Gospel to the Germanic tribes of Europe. He even got as far as choosing a team of helpers, obtaining a ship for the voyage and stocking it with food and other provisions. Then his plans were thwarted. First by one of the brethren who saw a vision of the abbot of Melrose, Boisil, instructing him to tell Egbert to abandon the venture and to go instead to the monastery at Iona to reprove the monks, "because their ploughs do not run straight and it is his duty to recall them to the right way." Secondly, the ship, anchored in the harbour, was subjected to a severe battering by a storm and most of the provisions were lost. Then Egbert recalled the words of Jonah, "for my sake this great tempest is upon you" and he abandoned his attempts to sail to Frisia. Eventually he went to Iona to persuade the community there to adopt the customs of the Roman Church.

Egbert never lost his concern for the pagan tribes of Europe and encouraged others to undertake missionary work among them. One of his companions was the priest Wictbert who, like Egbert, had lived for some years in Ireland, striving for perfection in his isolated hermitage. He decided to undertake the work which Egbert had been unable to do and went across to Frisia. He was there for only two years, his work being hindered by the opposition of King Radbod.

Then the task of preaching to the Frisians fell to Wilfrid's pupil, Willibrord. We have an outline of his work and achievements from the pen of Bede and to this we may add the *Life of Willibrord* by Alcuin, written about fifty years after Willibrord's death. Alcuin was a scholar of the school at York and later became one of its most eminent masters as well as librarian of the monastery. He was then appointed by Charlemagne to become master of the Palace School at

Aachen and figured prominently in the educational and cultural reform movement of the Frankish Empire. A request had been made for a biography of Willibrord by the abbot of Echternach where Willibrord had been the first abbot. Echternach was fifty miles or so south of Aachen between the rivers Rhine and Meuse. Alcuin was suitable for the task of writing the biography not only because of his learning but because he was a fellow-Northumbrian of Willibrord and related to him. In the biography he states that he is a lawful inheritor of an estate and its small monastery which had belonged to Willibrord's father, Wilgils. The estate was on the bleak headland jutting out from the Humber estuary, now Spurn Head.

Alcuin follows the traditional pattern of contemporary Saint's Lives describing the supernatural portents surrounding Willibrord's birth. At the time of his conception, his mother had dreams, so strange and vivid, that the next day she called in a priest, blessed with prophetic powers, to interpret them. At once he foresaw the future greatness of the child the woman was to bear. He would dispel the darkness of error with the light of truth and draw the attention of many people by the beauty of his life and the dazzling brightness of his fame.

Willibrord was born in about 658 of noble Christian parents. The introduction into Anglo-Saxon society of Christian missionaries, almost all of whom were monks, brought with it an enthusiasm for monasticism. Monastic establishments small and large, for men, for women, or for both, were founded all over England and hermitages and anchorites' cells were built by pious laymen. Willibrord's father, Wilgils, when his parental responsibilities were over, built a cell on the estate he had received by royal grant at Spurn Head. Soon he attracted a group of devoted followers who shared with him the monastic life. Here he remained until his death and here he was buried.

When Willibrord had passed his infancy he was handed over to Bishop Wilfrid who governed a monastery at Ripon. Willibrord's gifts of character and intellect blossomed most wonderfully though he was frail and delicate in body. At fifteen he received the monastic tonsure, remaining at Ripon until he was twenty. Then, like many other Englishmen at that time, he accepted the hospitality and training offered by Irish monasteries. The year was 678 and at about this time Wilfrid was leaving England for Rome, wintering in Frisia. Perhaps his departure from Ripon prompted Willibrord's move to Ireland. He was there for about twelve years, studying, visiting masters of the spiritual life and striving to emulate their austerities and devotion. It was while he was in Ireland that he witnessed the extraordinary recovery from the plague of an Irish scholar who was given water to drink, into which a relic of the saintly King Oswald had been immersed. Later, when Willibrord was archbishop of the Frisians, he related this miracle to Wilfrid and to Acca who were visiting him at the time. The cult of St Oswald was as popular on the Continent as in England or Ireland. Willibrord had relics of the king in Frisia and there are records of other such relics being venerated in France, Belgium, Germany and northern Italy as well as many churches being dedicated to him.

The Celtic preoccupation with personal salvation which Willibrord found so many engaged upon in Ireland began to lose its appeal for him. He wished to spend his life in the service of others and in bringing Christianity to those in ignorance of it. He would follow, he thought, in the footsteps of Wilfrid who had preached to the heathen people of Frisia. He would take up the task where Wictbert had laid it down and carry out the work which Bishop Egbert had hoped to do himself. The project was fully discussed with the two men and in 690 Willibrord, with eleven companions, who were to share in his work, set sail for the Continent. They arrived at the mouth of the Rhine, disembarked and made their way to the old fortified city of Utrecht in western Frisia. Willibrord presented himself at the court of Pippin II, Mayor of the Palace of Austrasia, whom Alcuin describes as "a man of immense energy, successful in war and of high moral character." Pippin was quick to see the advantage of having a man of Willibrord's calibre at work among his people and those of neighbouring tribes. He was in favour of the conversion of the Frisians, those in the west now being under his control, and he readily gave Willibrord his support and protection. Utrecht, with grants of land and property from Pippin, became Willibrord's headquarters. Later when he was consecrated archbishop of the Frisians it was to be his episcopal seat.

But before embarking upon his task of evangelising the heathen Willibrord wished to place his work under the authority of Rome and to gain the approval and blessing of the pope, Sergius (687-701). Willibrord had been brought up and trained under the watchful eye of Wilfrid, one of England's most ardent supporters of Rome and twice a pilgrim to the Holy City. The English Church, though never losing its national identity, was modelled on that of Rome in its organisation, discipline and worship. Theodore, archbishop of Canterbury, had brought unity and order into the Church, increasing the number of dioceses and consecrating more bishops to serve in them. He had introduced the practice of annual synods, corrected abuses wherever he found them, urged the use of Roman customs and encouraged learning by means of his school at Canterbury. Against this background Willibrord had grown up, so the ideas he had absorbed were carried with him to the new lands he planned to evangelize.

No episcopal ordination was bestowed upon Willibrord on his first visit to Rome. Such an action would have been precipitate on the part of the pope. He wished first to watch the progress of the mission in Frisia, to mark Willibrord's powers of organisation and leadership and to test his character in face of trials and hardship. Willibrord was still in priest's orders, then, when he returned to Frisia.

Whether his return was delayed or whether he had not yet emerged as leader of the band of missionary monks we cannot say. But in his absence his companions took the decision to send one of their number to England to be made a bishop. They chose Swidbert, "a meek-hearted man of sober ways." He must have possessed gifts of character and intellect which commended him to his fellows. Perhaps some preferred him to Willibrord, though later when Pippin wished to have Willibrord consecrated archbishop, the brethren supported the choice. The consecration of Swidbert must have been quite in order since it was carried out by Wilfrid, a strict observer of ecclesiastical protocol. It seems, however, that Swidbert did not have the qualities of character and the powers of leadership required of a bishop and his episcopate was of short duration. He stayed in Frisia for a while, then went to preach to the heathen Bructeri in southern Westphalia. His work was halted by the invasions of the Old Saxons and the defeat of the Bructeri. Those he had converted were scattered and he was forced to retire to an island retreat on the Rhine, now Kaiserworth, given to him by Pippin. Here he lived a quiet and austere life until his death in 714. His relics are still preserved in the thirteenth century church on the site of the monastery he built there.

At about this time two English priests, both named Hewald, arrived in Old Saxony, intent upon converting the pagan people of that province. They were given hospitality by a local reeve who promised to conduct them to the chieftain who ruled over that area. But when the local inhabitants heard of the priests' whereabouts they put them both to death, one by the sword, the other torn limb from limb. Then they threw their bodies into the Rhine. The chieftain, angry at the savage cruelty of these men, ordered them to be slain and all the villagers with them and their village burned. The two Hewalds were given honourable burial as befits martyrs and later, when Pippin heard of this terrible atrocity, he directed that the bodies of the two martyrs should be transferred to the church in the city of Cologne.

Willibrord, now the undisputed leader of the Frisian mission, began in earnest the task of evangelizing the heathen. For several years he and his fellow monks travelled round western Frisia preaching, baptising and founding churches. Many turned away from their idolatrous worship and accepted the Faith of Christ. So fruitful was their work that Pippin decided to send Willibrord to Rome to be consecrated archbishop of Frisia. The consecration took place on 21st November, 695. The date is recorded in an early eighth century calendar, now in the National Library in Paris, believed to have belonged to Willibrord, the date entered in his own hand. On the occasion of the consecration Pope Sergius gave Willibrord the name of Clement.

Willibrord returned to Utrecht which now became his episcopal seat. An imposing statue of Willibrord in today's city centre reminds local inhabitants of the Englishman who brought Christianity to Holland and became its patron saint. At the time of his consecration he was still a young man of about thirty-seven and had many years of missionary work in front of him. With the help of his companions he saw that Christianity was preached all over western Frisia; pagan shrines were destroyed and churches built. In Utrecht Willibrord built a cathedral church and dedicated it to Christ the Saviour; a second church in Utrecht was dedicated to St Martin, a popular saint at the time. W. Levison in his book *England and the Continent in the Eighth Century* has reminded us that identical dedications existed both in Rome and in Canterbury. Thus Willibrord was linking his newly formed Church in Frisia with the Church of Rome and that of Canterbury.

Willibrord was a man of adventurous and courageous spirit. His evangelistic zeal took him beyond western Frisia into alien country outside of Pippin's protection. He went first into Radbod's territory, independent Frisia, and obtained an audience with the king. On this occasion Radbod received him with unexpected kindness but his opposition to Christian missionary enterprise was unchanged. He forbade Willibrord to preach in his kingdom.

Willibrord turned now to the fierce tribes of Denmark whose king, Ongendus, Alcuin describes as "more savage than any wild beast and harder than stone." Like Radbod he was devoted to his own pagan faith and way of life and refused Willibrord permission to preach. Willibrord did, however, manage to bring out of the country thirty young men whom he instructed in the Christian faith and baptised. We assume that he brought them back to Frisia for further training with the expectation that they would return to their own land to preach to their people; but we hear no more of them.

On the return journey to Frisia Willibrord's ship ran into a fierce storm and was driven onto the island of Heligoland. It was then called Frositeland after the local god, Frosite, whom all the local inhabitants worshipped with awe and dread: they must do nothing they believed, to anger their god. Water from the sacred springs must only be drawn in utter silence and the sacred cows that roamed the hillside must be left untouched, providing the people with neither milk nor meat. Willibrord fearlessly preached to these superstitious people, scorned their pagan customs and delivered them from the bondage of their fears. Using water from the sacred well and speaking loud and strong the name of the Holy Trinity he baptised three of their number. Then he ordered cattle to be killed to feed himself and his company. When Radbod, in whose kingdom the island lay, heard of Willibrord's insult to their gods, he sent for him and, in a furious rage, demanded to know why he had violated their sacred customs. Willibrord, though in danger of losing his life, defended his actions and preached the way of truth to the king. Radbod, though rejecting Willibrord's message, was impressed by his composure and sent him back to Pippin unharmed.

Both Alcuin and Bede tell us of monasteries founded by Willibrord. The most famous of these was at Echternach between the Rhine and the Meuse in what is today Luxemburg. The land was given jointly by an abbess of Trier, near Echternach, and by King Pippin who greatly enriched the monastery with gifts. The beautiful manuscripts of the Gospels, The Echternach Gospels, now in the National Library in Paris, once belonged to Willibrord's monastery. Because of their resemblance to the Lindisfarne Gospels they are thought to have been written in Northumbria by a Northumbrian scribe, perhaps at Lindisfarne itself, and then taken to Echternach for use in the monastery there. Alternatively they could have been written by a Northumbrian scribe at Echternach, perhaps by one of Willibrord's original companions.

In 714 Willibrord's patron, Pippin II of Heristal, died, plunging the Frankish kingdom for several years into turmoil and causing a temporary setback in church affairs. Pippin's widow, Plectrudis, a woman of domineering personality, desired power for herself and her grandson. She therefore threw into prison Pippin's most obvious successor, his son Charles Martel, borne by his concubine Alphaida. The internal struggle for power weakened the Frankish kingdom and presented an opportunity for neighbouring tribes to regain their lost territories. Neustria, the western province of the Frankish kingdom, saw no future with Plectrudis and her grandson in power and therefore attacked Austrasia, the ruling province. The Neustrians were joined by Radbod of Frisia, Old Saxony and Burgundy. Radbod regained his hold over Frankish Frisia, drove out the Christian missionaries, destroyed churches and re-established pagan worship. Willibrord had to leave his episcopal seat at Utrecht and retire to his monastery at Echternach. We have seen that it was during this period of political upheaval that Boniface arrived in Frisia but was obliged to leave and return home until the situation stabilized.

The shape of European history might have been quite different if Pippin's son, Charles, had not escaped from prison and taken command of Austrasian forces against the rebellious uprisers, in particular those of Neustria. After a series of unsuccessful campaigns against them, Charles had, by 719, became ruler of Austrasia, Neustria, the whole of Frisia, Burgundy and other neighbouring tribes. In all but name, and with great popular support, he was virtually king of Frankland. As a patron of the Church he restored Willibrord to his episcopal seat at Utrecht and offered him his protection. Willibrord set about rebuilding the churches Radbod had destroyed and restoring Christian worship. He was assisted now by Boniface who had come out once more to preach to the heathen.

Alcuin tells us very little about Willibrord's work between 719 and his death in 739. He extols his virtues, describes his appearance and relates a number of miracles attributed to him. "Now this holy man was distinguished by every kind of natural quality: he was of middle height, dignified mien, comely of face, cheerful of spirit, wise in counsel, pleasing in speech, grave in character and energetic in everything he undertook for God." Of the miracles, Alcuin says that they are not to be considered as important as Willibrord's preaching of the Gospel; they are included in his biography for the glory of God and the interest of future generations. He tells how Willibrord suffered no harm when he was struck on the head by an irate custodian of a pagan shrine; how an outbreak of plague in a nunnery subsided when he gave water, blessed by himself, to the nuns to drink; how the wine in his flagon was undiminished after he had given twelve beggars drink from it; and how he deprived, and later restored, a man's ability to swallow after he had uttered curses upon Willibrord and his company and refused to drink with them.

The power of prophecy, too, belonged to Willibrord and was shown when he baptized the infant son of Charles Martel, Pippin. "Know that this child will be highly exalted and renowned. He will be greater than all the kings of the Franks who have gone before him", said Willibrord. His prophecy was indeed fulfilled when Pippin III (the Short) was anointed king by archbishop Boniface. He ruled the Franks with wisdom and insight, laying the foundation for the work of his more famous son, Charlemagne.

When Bede was finishing his *History of the English Church and People* in 731 Willibrord was still alive. Speaking of his mission in Frisia Bede says, "he appointed a number of bishops, choosing them from among the brethren who had come with him, or after him, to preach. Some of these have now fallen asleep in the Lord, but Willibrord himself, surnamed Clement, is still living, and is much revered for his great age. He has been thirty-six years a bishop, and after the countless spiritual battles he has fought, longs with all his heart for the prize of a heavenly reward." Bede himself died in 735 and Willibrord four years later, in November 739. He died at the monastery at Echternach, aged eighty-one and was buried there. "He it was," says Boniface in a letter to Pope Stephen III about the Frisian people, "who converted them to the faith of Christ."

Bibliography

Primary Sources

The Anglo-Saxon Chronicle. Translated G. M. Garmonsway. 1960
Bede's Ecclesiastical History
  1. Edited and translated B. Colgrave and R. A. B. Mynors. 1969
  2. Translated L. Sherley-Price. Penguin Classics. Revised 1970
  3. Latin text and notes. C. Plummer. 1896
English Historical Documents. Volume 1. Revised 1979
The Anglo-Saxon Missionaries in Germany. C. H. Talbot. 1954
Lives of the Saints. Translated by J. F. Webb. Penguin Classics. 1965

The Anglo-Saxons

Hodgkin, R. K. *A History of the Anglo-Saxons.* 1952
Hunter-Blair, P. *An Introduction to Anglo-Saxon England.* 1956
Loyn, H. R. *Anglo-Saxon England and the Norman Conquest.* 1962
Page, R. I. *Life in Anglo-Saxon England.* 1970
Stenton, F. *Anglo-Saxon England.* 1947
Whitelock, D. *The Beginnings of English Society.* 1952

The Church

Deanesly, M. *The Pre-Conquest Church in England.* 1963
Duckett, E. *Anglo-Saxon Saints and Scholars.* 1947
Field, J. E. *St Berin, Apostle of Wessex.*
Godfrey, C. J. *The Church in Anglo-Saxon England.* 1962
Hunter-Blair, P. *The World of Bede.* 1970
Mayr-Harting, H. *The Coming of Christianity to Anglo-Saxon England.* 1972

The Continent

Albertson, C. *Anglo-Saxon Saints and Heroes.* 1967
Crawford, S. J. *Anglo-Saxon Influence on Western Christendom.* 1966
Kylie, E. *The English Correspondence of St Boniface.* 1911
Lasko, P. *The Kingdom of the Franks.* 1971
Levison, W. *England and the Continent in the eighth Century.* 1946

Index